LEARN TO SEE

"Learn to See is an exceptionally clear, practical and insightful guide to accessing one's Higher Self. The exercises in the book are extremely useful and easy to follow."

—Nicki Weiss, author

"In *Learn to See*, we are given the tools to look within—to see beyond our everyday lives, to see the impact we make on others, and they on us."

—Joan M. Coles, co-author,
Emily Post Talks with Teens about Manners and Etiquette

"Learn to See is fabulous—it provides an incredibly easy way to understand what the universe is trying to tell us in our life. Mary Jo McCabe is a master at explaining things people have been pondering for decades. She is truly a leader on the forefront of a new evolution of personal growth and development."

—Bonnie Young, Marketing Expert

"On our journey to spiritual enlightenment, we pass through many doors. Mary Jo McCabe's extraordinary gifts, communicated to us so clearly through Ed Greer's masterful style, has opened a door to us, whose threshold, once crossed, will change your life forever and bring you a giant step closer to full and open communication with the Universal Spirit."

—John Odom, President,
Aries Financial Management, Inc.

"Our maturation to adulthood all too often involves learning to stifle our intuition and awareness of our innermost guidance. Trained as a medical doctor, with great respect for scientific proof, I was woefully out of touch with these areas of myself. Through the exercises in this book, I have attained the self-awareness, spontaneity, and open communication with my higher self to know what I want and how to grow.

"*Learn to See* can help you unlock the pathways to receive the direction you need. And rather than having you merely read about how to do it, Mary Jo takes you through the doing of it."

—William E. Callahan, Jr., M.D., psychiatrist,
San Clemente, CA

"In our busy world and our busy lives, we all need time to slow down and to connect with our higher power and inner light. *Learn to See* gives us a roadmap, a way to get there."

—Dr. Laura L'Herisson, psychologist

LEARN
TO
SEE

*An Approach to
Your Inner Voice
Through Symbols*

MARY JO McCABE
Written with L. Edwin Greer

Blue Dolphin Publishing
1994

Copyright © 1994 Mary Jo McCabe

g, Inc.

ISBN# 0-931892-86-4

Library of Congress Cataloging-in-Publication Data

McCabe, Mary Jo, 1947–
    Learn to see : an approach to your inner voice through symbols
/ Mary Jo McCabe ; written with Edwin Greer.
        p.   cm.
    Includes bibliographical references.
    ISBN 0-931892-86-4 : $11.00
    1. Spiritual life.   2. Symbolism.   I. Greer, Edwin.   II. Title.
BL624.M395 1994
131—dc20   94-16622
                                                     CIP

Cover art: Tom Byg

Printed in the United States of America by
Blue Dolphin Press, Inc., Grass Valley, California

10   9   8   7   6   5   4   3   2

Table of Contents

Foreword

Mary Jo McCabe has gained a wide following over the past decade, having astounded more than ten thousand people throughout the country with the accuracy and relevance of her spiritual readings.

This book discusses Mary Jo's unique talent and, more importantly, reveals how the reader can develop his or her own gift of insight.

Learn to See opens the way to receiving direct messages from your Higher Self and contains specific exercises that one can use on a daily basis to identify and interpret symbols that provide direction to our lives. It explores the relationship that exists among all facets of the universe and enables the reader to expand his awareness immeasurably.

Mary Jo and a group of volunteers developed these techniques over several years of work and actual application. I have been unable to find any other book today that provides such hands-on exercises for the expansion of our awareness and insight. These techniques have practical, day-to-day application, as well as being fun to try. People who have participated in her workshops with these exercises have experienced surprising results.

Through this book we have sought to combine Mary Jo's proven techniques for greater awareness with her natural excitement for life.

I believe *Learn to See* will provide compelling insights into the Higher Self and become a practical, day-to-day guide to making effective choices through symbols.

—L. Edwin Greer

Introduction

At the age of thirty-four I was propelled into an atmosphere no astronaut had ever explored. It was not charted on any map and beyond the reach of any compass. My direction was from a group of souls I have come to know as "The Guides." I had never seen them, and they had never told me my destination. Yet to miss the trip was unthinkable.

I began this journey in 1981. In the years that followed, I have explored and learned to use my gift of reading the souls of others. I have shared the secrets of 10,000 souls. It has been both exhilarating and terrifying to look beyond the shoebox that we think defines our lives and see the real events, both past and future, which have molded today.

Although I am told there is a ripple effect among family and friends, my work is with the individual. I spend a period of time sharing with a person a photo album of his soul. Together we turn the pages, looking back into other lives in other centuries and then forward for a glimpse of yet to be experienced successes and failures. But most important are the pages of today. Both the past and the future have their indelible imprints on today.

So my Guides turn the pages and through my voice describe the photographs that reveal the soul. And the exciting thing is that every person is the caretaker of a colorful, curious and exciting soul. Even better, you don't need me to experience the dimensions of your soul. This book has been written to enable you to become more fully aware of exactly who you are, and to open to you the worlds of knowledge available to you. There is a library of limitless knowledge waiting for you. This is your key to the door of that library.

CHAPTER 1

The Whisper of Truth

Truth whispers down through the centuries
to embrace the soul.

There is a truth which pulses through the universe, connecting all time and all people. This truth is available to you if you open yourself to it. It will help you to understand yourself and your place in this world. It will help in understanding those who are in this life with you. It can provide guidance in making day-to-day choices as well as long term, life path decisions. This current of truth can give you a depth of awareness and understanding beyond anything you thought possible.

Michelangelo once had been commissioned to carve a statue in a courtyard. A young boy came by and watched him begin to chisel the huge stone for a moment. Then the puzzled boy asked the great sculptor why he was hitting at that rock. Michelangelo replied, "Because there's an angel inside, and it wants to come out." There is an angel inside you, pressing against the windowpane of your consciousness, wanting to get out and lead you in your quest for life.

All we need is a method of releasing this angel within. The use of symbols from your higher self is the key to

unlocking this wealth of timeless information and awareness.

This is a logical part of God's plan. We were not put
here to struggle in isolation. We have not been asked to
live out a lifespan of seven decades, limited to what little
we can learn and retain in that short time. Are we not
expected to build on what has occurred before us? May we
not be permitted some insight into what the future holds?

We are related in spirit to others who sit at our table
and who pass us on the street. We are related to those who
have stood on these same sands in other years and other
centuries. There is a connection with those who will follow
us. The past, present and future are not found through
doors off a single chronological hallway of time. When we
come to understand fully the concept of time, we shall be
able to move readily from one segment of time into another.

Knowledge brings freedom—freedom from the invisible bonds of this existence. In ignorance we build walls.
With knowledge we build bridges. Without an awareness
of what there is to be discovered beyond the immediate
horizon, we imprison ourselves in a limited world. We
limit our capacity for growth and fulfillment. When one's
world is circumscribed by frantic activities directed toward keeping the body fed and clothed and acquiring an
appropriate number and style of material possessions,
life's potential is missed. Our world has a tendency to
entangle us in routine. Much of our daily energy is con-
sumed in carrying out the routine duties life has assigned
us, duties which absorb our time but yield no meaning to
our lives. Wages must be earned. Bills must be paid. We do
what we must do so that we along with our families may
proceed to the next day with our relationships and possessions intact. We are pushed to fill our day with routine that

is repeated again and again, leaving little room for contemplative thought or growth. The daily barrage of bills, sales promotions and other demands does not encourage inner growth.

In the succeeding chapters I show you how to reach your life's potential by unlocking the passageway that joins the conscious self with the higher self. I urge you to take advantage of the knowledge, truth and awareness that lie on the other side of that invisible door.

Knowledge gives man perspective. Understanding the relationship of the past and the future gives man purpose in the present. Awareness of the past and the future is available to us today. We open our minds to this library of knowledge by learning to communicate with our higher selves. Communication is our passport. It is the means of clearing away the mist that hangs over us, limiting our access to this information that awaits our call.

Before going further, take a moment to visualize a clock of any type. It may be a typical round-faced clock or a digital timepiece. What time do you see on your clock at this moment? Remember this time. I shall explain its significance in a later chapter.

CHAPTER 2

The Message of Symbols

The symbol plucks all the strings of the human spirit
at once . . .

J. J. Bachofen

The vast universe of truth and knowledge is available to us through communication with our higher selves. You may refer to this higher self by any one of a number of names—your inner God, your unconscious, your intuition, your small voice within. By whatever name, each of us has an inner guidance that has access to all the knowledge we shall ever need or could ever use.

This inner guidance speaks to us through symbols transmitted to our consciousness. The symbols are waiting, have been waiting for centuries, like a movie script waiting to be opened and read and spoken. As these symbols are allowed to march across our minds, they bring to us a new depth of awareness.

Visualizing symbols is the most natural means of learning. This is the way our brains send us messages. We don't think in terms of lines of words on a piece of paper. We think in illustrations or images. It is therefore natural for your higher self to transmit concepts to you in images as well.

4

It is important to be aware of the relationship between symbols and communication. We seldom give much thought to the prominent role that symbols play in our daily lives. In fact, there is no more pervasive influence on our movement from one hour to the next and one day to the next than the direction, stimulation and security that we receive from various forms of symbols. Symbols are indeed much more than the advertising logos found on the myriad of commercial products being constantly thrust at us.

Symbols operate at every level of our existence. Susanne K. Langer in *Philosophy in a New Key: A Study in the Symbolism of Reason, Rite and Art*, finds the need of symbolization to be a basic need of man and the power of using symbols to be the principal factor behind his pre-eminence on this earth. She writes:

> The symbol-making function is one of man's primary activities, like eating, looking, or moving about. It is the fundamental process of his mind, and goes on all the time. Sometimes we are aware of it, sometimes we merely find its results, and realize that certain experiences have passed through our brains and have been digested there.

Professor A. D. Ritchey points out in *The Natural History of the Mind* that symbolization is the essential act of thought.

In *Symbols, Signs and Their Meaning*, Arnold Whittick agrees with the vital role that symbols play in our lives. He states:

> Civilization, the process of man's development beyond mere animal existence, has been achieved largely by his

ability to use and invent symbols. Communication depends on the symbolism of language, and thus man becomes aware of another's thought by means of symbols. By language combined with his propensity to dream, plan and speculate, which is in part a further type of symbolism, man extends his thought beyond his own time and place, a detachment indispensible to the enlargement of his activities.

On a superficial level symbols announce who we are through the style and color of our clothing and the type of automobile we drive. Our structures are frequently built to symbolize their functions. Bank buildings convey the impression of stability. Courtrooms suggest austere dignity. Our entire economic system rests on the symbolism of pieces of green paper and plastic cards.

A symphony orchestra is able to reproduce the musical visions of Mozart because he memorialized those visions in symbols. Every religion of the world relies heavily on symbols that are passed down from generation to generation. Our most personal relationships are symbolized by a ring and symbolic promises to love, honor and obey.

But symbols go far beyond this to the most fundamental levels of our existence. Symbols become the mental signposts which give us perspective on time and space. We have symbolically divided our days into hours, minutes and seconds in order to give us some footholds on time. We can thus measure progress, set schedules and coordinate our lives with those of others. We need to have a yardstick to comprehend how far we have traveled on life's excursion. Each measurement is a symbol. In the same manner we measure space through symbols of distance. Only in this way are we able to acclimate ourselves geographically.

Thus, we literally define our lives through symbols. As suggested by S. I. Hayakawa in *Symbol, Status and Personality*, even the individual who believes himself to be in direct contact with reality thinks in terms of the symbols which he has been taught to organize his perceptions. Joseph L. Henderson in *Man and His Symbols*, edited by Carl Jung, stated:

> [The symbol-making capacity of the unconscious mind of modern man] still plays a role of vital psychic importance. In more ways than we realize, we are dependent on the messages that are carried by such symbols, and both our attitudes and our behavior are profoundly influenced by them.

Symbols are the basis of our accumulation of knowledge and advancement as a civilization. In fact, we have become so adept at the formulation and recognition of symbols that we often overlook the fact that we are so dependent upon this ability.

CHAPTER 3

A Symbolic Vocabulary

*An idea, in the highest sense of that word, cannot be
conveyed but by a symbol.*

Samuel Taylor Coleridge

Nowhere do symbols play a more vital role than in communication. It is thus appropriate that symbols should form the basis for communication with your higher self. Your higher self directs images to you. These images are symbols which represent specific messages.

In using symbols it is necessary to agree on the meaning each symbol will carry. This is true in any communication. Both ends of the communicative process must come to an agreement that a particular symbol hereafter will stand for a particular message. Indeed, this is the way every language in use today had its birth. Symbols were selected to represent different ideas or objects. The Chinese drew this relationship even closer by designing symbols in their language which resembled the objects they signified. The present Chinese character for woman is a direct descendent of the pictogram in which a woman was depicted as a sort of stick figure with arms and legs. The symbol for man was a slight variation of that image.

Thus, instead of developing an alphabet with letters combined to form words with assigned arbitrary meanings, the Chinese collected actual visual images until their language reached six to eight thousand characters in common use. Dennis Bloodworth tells us in *The Chinese Looking Glass* that an ordinary Chinese typewriter had 2,590 keys plus blank settings for the insertion of 3,432 rarer characters as needed. The Chinese language is perhaps the most obvious example of communication based upon symbols tied directly to the appearance of the objects they represent.

The entire process of written communication is based upon symbols. Richard Lederer in *The Miracle of Language* marvels at the fact that a reader is able to experience ideas similar to those the writer thought while putting down the written symbols in another place and another time. He says:

> Because I write and you read, we can both extend ourselves beyond the creatures we each were when we were born and the people we each were before I began the writing and you the reading.

The only way for you to begin to communicate with your higher self is to develop a language constructed of symbols. You will need your own personal vocabulary. As this vocabulary is worked out, each time an image is projected to you by your higher self, it will represent the same object or idea that it did the time before.

It does not ultimately matter what symbol you find to be fitting to represent a particular concept. To take a simple example, if the term "larger than life" evokes the image of an elephant to you, this may be a useful symbol for that idea. Someone else might relate more readily to an image of the Empire State Building. Another might mentally see a giant when using that phrase. One image is as

valid as another as long as it feels right to you. The point is
for you and your higher or inner self to agree upon your
symbolic vocabulary.

I do not want to leave the impression, however, that
the symbols which form the basis for communication
between your consciousness and your higher self are
arbitrarily selected. Although it does not matter what the
symbol is, the particular image that is projected onto your
mental movie screen will have a special meaning for you
and your higher self. It will have some type of emotional
content for you. Often it will carry a universal message or
perhaps a message that has a uniform meaning to all
members of a particular culture. For example, according
to many cultural traditions, white is symbolic of purity. If
you and I share the same cultural background, then a
number of your symbols should correlate very closely
with mine. Other symbols may reflect your personal experiences in life. These will be personal to you and possibly
without meaning to anyone else. However, any symbol
that speaks to you is valid.

Your personal symbols will be the vocabulary between your higher self and the conscious part of your
being that goes about life in your external world. They will
change the focus of your world.

Here is a brief exercise that I find to be very revealing,
one which you can use to gain an immediate personal
symbol for your new vocabulary. Close your fingers into a
fist. Relax your mind and body. Then slowly open your
hand and visualize in your palm the first object that comes
to mind. It can be anything. My clients have seen money,
automobiles, crowns and everything else imaginable. We
shall come back to the relevance of this exercise as we
explore more about the meaning of symbols.

CHAPTER 4

Listen As a Child

We come through the door of skepticism into
the treasure house of mystery.
Henry Thomas, Dana Lee Thomas

"Once upon a time in a land far, far away, there lived a handsome prince . . ." These words once invited many of us into a land of enchantment. We walked down this word path willing to yield our senses to whatever excitement and magic this unknown world had to offer. But it counted only if we were there to believe. Disbelief was not a part of the child's world. So—while the winter chill clothed the remaining leaves of winter with ice outside, we were warm in the anticipation of the excitement that awaited us. We walked into the pages to see what was happening in the castle that day. We were part of the story.

It is helpful today to stretch back to those childhood days and approach your higher self from the viewpoint of a child. This is a constructive technique in becoming open to life's symbols.

It seems that childhood brings with it a purity of thought that we suppress more and more as we stack up the layers of years in becoming an adult. As we move through life, we construct for ourselves a suit of armor that is intended to protect us and express who we are. In medieval times knights hoped their uniforms of mail and iron conveyed a sense of the invincible as they went into battle. They believed this heavy and bulky garment protected them from their adversaries' blows and projected an attitude of power and invincibility.

For exactly the same reasons we today cover ourselves year by year with a mental suit of armor in the belief that it shields us from the arrows of insult and criticism and conveys a proper image—that we are who we are "supposed to be." In doing so we trap and confine ourselves. We hide the true self behind this wall of mental mail and iron. We gain a certain security, but we do so at the cost of wholeness to our personality. As we block out the pain, we also limit the pleasure. This limits, as well, our ability to show love and compassion. We inhibit our ability to feel.

Multiply this by most of the earth's population and you have a world of trapped personalities clanking around the earth in self-imposed suits of mental iron. We communicate only to the extent our mental shackles permit, allowing little of the unique and spontaneous personality either out or in.

When one here or there senses a desire for throwing off this confinement and seeking the whole self, we can do this only by freeing the unconscious. And we can best free the potential that lies there by returning to the thought mode of the child that existed before we took on this restricting armor.

Carl Jung has written about the clarity with which a child views himself and the world. Jung has said that:

> . . . a characteristic of childhood is that, thanks to its naivete and unconsciousness, it sketches a more com-

plete picture of the self, of the whole man in his pure individuality, than adulthood. Consequently, the sight of a child or a primitive will arouse certain longings in adult, civilized persons—longings which relate to the unfulfilled desires and needs of those parts of the personality which have been blotted out of the total picture in favor of the adapted persona.

Jung expressed concern that a part of his own personality had become invisible under the influence and pressure of his culture.

So a technique for setting the stage for clear communication with your inner being is to think back to those carefree days of childhood and listen for the inner voice with the innocence of a child. Perhaps recall lying in the soft grass watching the clouds move across a summer sky. Anything was possible then. Anything is possible now. It is waiting for you!

. . . And they lived happily ever after.

CHAPTER 5

Why Me?

*Indeed, our day-to-day thoughts and wishes and actions are
but a small surface demonstration of the potential
resources in the vast warehouse of our subconscious.*
Henry Lee Thomas, Dana Lee Thomas

How did all this begin? To understand these concepts
fully, we should look briefly at their origin in my own life.
Although I am an enthusiastic bearer of this message
today, I suppose I was a reluctant student years ago when
I first stood before the blackboard of symbology. I was
assuming my role as the wife of an Air Force navigator
and the mother of a young son when a certain insistent
prodding kept forcing its way into my consciousness. I
knew I occasionally dreamed of events before they occurred, hearing my dream reported to me on the morning
news the next day. However, I pushed these and other
unusual events aside, not wishing to reshape my life in
midstream.

In 1980 I finally began to heed an inner voice that had
become more and more insistent. I was receiving visions
which were increasing both in number and intensity.
Something inside me was demanding expression. I came
to realize I could not rest until I had answered this knock.

I awoke one morning and recalled a vivid dream about the Falkland Islands, a place unfamiliar to me. I had seen people running on a ship. I told my husband, Jim, that I had dreamed there would be an explosion or bombing on a ship. I related my dream of seeing people screaming and running. We finished our breakfast and I left to run my morning errands without opening the newspaper. Later on a neighbor came over and brought up the subject of an attack on the Falkland Islands. I ran to get our paper and saw my dream reported in the most accurate detail on the front page!

By this time I had waded into the shallow end of the metaphysical pool. I felt I was getting into the flow of something, and the current was definitely taking me with it whether I wanted to go or not.

A New Life's Work

My work as interpreter for the Guides soon absorbed my life. I could not easily explain my work to others. Here I was, a sane, rational housewife and mother, sitting and watching these symbols being projected onto the screen of my mind by some beings called the Guides, most of whom I had yet to see. Other mothers were scout den mothers and charity event organizers. My son, Bhrett, couldn't even tell his friends what his mom did each day.

By 1987 I was communicating with the Guides almost as much as I was talking with my friends and family. My work became all I thought about and talked about. It kept gaining momentum.

People were calling me from all over the country. I did not know most of these people and did not know how they had heard of me. I was certainly not publicizing my gift and had been told by the Guides that I should interpret only for those who sought me out as only they would be ready for the information available to them. So my telephone rang increasingly at all hours of the day and night.

People called seeking a better understanding of themselves and their purpose on this earth. I was able to look into their souls and tell them about themselves and others. Together we were able to find the causes of problems, both internal and in relationships with those close to them.

In order to accommodate more people as well as explore other aspects of the higher self in a group setting, in 1989 I scheduled a retreat at an old plantation home called Asphodel Plantation. Located in a historic corner of Louisiana, this old mansion still has all the charm of a century and a half ago, when, at the end of a successful cotton harvest, the music from the ballroom blended with the tunes of the crickets outside.

This was an exciting time for me. I had endured the labors of the Guides' education. My days were filled with personal readings. Now I would spend a whole weekend with a group of people stretching to the limits of their souls. I felt I had finally reached my purpose in this work and in life. I did not know what the weekend held in store, but I knew it would be exciting.

On Friday evening I went to the conference room before the others arrived. I was acutely aware that I had the responsibility of a large group of people, each of whom had paid some $300 for the weekend. The response had been good, and I was exhilarated that they had such confidence in me.

As I entered the meeting room, I was struck by a message broadly scrawled across the blackboard.

"IF THE STUDENT FAILS TO LEARN,
THE TEACHER HAS FAILED TO TEACH."

It was undoubtedly a message from the Guides. Sometimes I think their primary focus is keeping my humility level at its highest peak.

With my ego properly cautioned, I found the retreat meaningful and successful. The Guides taught lessons of love and acceptance, and each person was able to look deeply within himself. I believe that relationships became closer and individuals more inspired about their futures.

This retreat emphasized my belief that my gift of communication is meant to operate on a personal level. Although I may receive insight concerning worldwide events from time to time, the significance of such events is the impact they may have on the personal life of the person before me. My mission is to help the individual gain personal insight into his life and his talents. My purpose is to open the individual to love and acceptance. Nations may rise and fall, but international shifts of power in this lifetime are less important than the growth of the eternal soul.

In the few years following the Asphodel retreat I have conducted seminars, workshops and retreats on a regular basis. I have continued to schedule individual readings for people both at my office and by telephone. I have published a series of booklets of teachings by the Guides and have a small library of tapes consisting of teachings on a wide range of subjects.

I have done more than 10,000 readings. Many have been for counselors and parents seeking to understand better their children and others important to their worlds. Most have been individuals who want a clearer understanding of who they are. They are looking to understand their purpose in this world and how to find more meaning in life. They hope to strengthen their relationship with their God.

In looking back over more than a decade, I see a collage of lives changing, shifting, awakening. Every day of that period involved some contact with the souls of others. I have learned that the Guides do not take vacations or observe holidays. I am only the translator, but there is a great personal reward for me in seeing the changes which insights from the Guides bring to people's lives.

Sometimes the change is dramatic, such as the lady who rushed up to me just before church one Sunday morning saying, "You saved my life!" She explained that a few months before, she had consulted her doctor about an abdominal pain. He found nothing and sent her back home. Later that evening the pain became more intense to the point of being almost unbearable. She again called her doctor, whose partner was then taking his calls. He agreed to see her. He too found nothing. The lady said she suddenly recalled a previous reading in which I had told her, "Watch your blood in July." It was July! She implored the doctor please to check her blood. He humored her and did so. She waited in pain for the results. The next thing she heard from the doctor was, "Oh, my God, your blood count is out of sight!" He called an ambulance and had her rushed to the hospital for removal of a ruptured appendix!

I more often hear stories of those who have been helped to steer clear of a destructive relationship or given the insight to launch a new career. One businessman in his forties said I had described to him a situation between him and his father that only the two of them knew about and which they had never discussed in thirty years. His reading brought this problem to light, promoting a long overdue solution.

A concerned young mother spoke emotionally of her twenty-year old son who was being sent to Saudi Arabia during the buildup for Desert Storm. She shared the fears of a mother in her most helpless hours. The Guides reassured her that he would return safely to her at the end of the war. They also told her she must prepare herself to share him, however, because upon his return he would become engaged to be married. When I next saw this mother at one of my workshops, she eagerly informed me that her son had returned safely exactly when the Guides said he would and had even telephoned ahead asking her to buy an engagement ring for him!

These and countless other experiences have confirmed that my gift has been given to me to open wider the minds of those who come to see me and to help them to begin a meaningful search on their own spiritual paths. I have also learned that part of my gift and my mission is to teach others to tap directly into the reservoir of awareness and knowledge about themselves and the world around them. This is the purpose of the lessons in this book.

CHAPTER 6

Thursday Night Guinea Pigs

Creative achievement is the boldest initiative of mind,
an adventure that takes its hero simultaneously to
the rim of knowledge and the limits of propriety.
Its pleasure is not the comfort of the safe harbor,
but the thrill of the reaching sail.

Robert Grudin

The exercises assembled for you in this book are the product of a twelve-year journey with the Guides. More specifically they are the crystallization of a year-long experiment with a group of students to develop a workable program by which anyone can communicate at any time with his or her higher self.

A group of twenty-two people, who dubbed themselves the "Thursday Night Guinea Pigs," met each week and explored how best to connect with the inner self. As one member recently put it, "The group laughed, cried and grew together on many levels as we journeyed into ourselves." Working sometimes individually, sometimes in pairs and at other times as an entire group, we explored, expanded, backed up and tried again until we found the most effective methods of bringing the higher self to the forefront.

The participants in this experimental group say they developed an inner awareness that they continue to experience on a daily basis. They credit the sessions with enhancing their spiritual lives and bringing them closer to their personal God. Most of them continue to emphasize how these sessions gave them focus, gave them a concrete method of dealing with problems of the day and changed their lives for the better.

After we had tried and honed many exercises, week after week and month after month, I combined the best of these into a one-day workshop that I have conducted in various cities. The workshops have enabled me to refine these techniques even further. This book is the culmination of years of dialogue with the Guides, the work of the Thursday Night Guinea Pigs and workshops teaching others the techniques of symbology. I hope your name may be added to the volumes of those who find their lives changed by these methods.

CHAPTER 7

Learning About Yourself

The psyche is in motion,
working in its nonconscious darkness to unfold
the patterns of experience by which the person can fulfill
the meaning of his individual life in the light of consciousness.
Ira Progroff

With the foundation of learning to communicate with our higher selves through symbols in mind, let's focus on you individually. Here are four preliminary exercises that will tell you something about yourself. They will show you where you presently stand on your spiritual journey through life as well as provide insight into your needs and methods of learning.

Merely relax and follow the brief directions as given. Accept the symbols you receive without passing judgment on them or editing them in any way. This is a preview of more extensive exercises to come later. The interpretations I have provided are the products of my years of exploration with the Guides. As you progress in this book, I show you how to recognize and interpret your own symbols. First, follow these exercises and gain additional insight into the person you are at this moment.

Frame Your Life

Close your eyes and visualize a picture frame. It can be as plain or as ornate as you wish. Make it either large or small. Leave the inside blank for a moment and color the frame itself with any color you choose. Next create a rose within your frame. Take a close look at the rose.

Now open your eyes. The color of your frame and details of your rose will tell you where you currently stand on your spiritual path in life.

INTERPRETATION: If your rose had opened, your learning has been intense. You have already completed much of your spiritual work. You have a new sense of freedom about yourself. If your rose was closed or still just budding, you are just starting to concentrate on your spiritual learning. This means you feel young in heart. You are excited about living your life.

The color of your frame will give you greater detail regarding your current spiritual learning.

Frame Color: *Interpretation:*

Blue

You are searching for peace and calm. You are trying to release fear.

Pink/Rose

You are learning to enjoy and live life. You feel blessed to be a part of the physical world.

Purple

You are learning to reach into the spiritual world. You are becoming one with all. You are now taking responsibility for yourself.

Gold/Yellow   You are learning to balance both the emo-
              tional and mental worlds.

White   You have burdens and responsibilities on
              you. With them comes your purpose in life,
              not fear. You can no longer face ignorance
              in your life path for you now know better.

Red   Caution! You have set your own bounda-
              ries. You must discipline yourself. Your
              need is to be heard by others.

Black   You are trying to quiet—or hide—shad-
              ows from your past. You are closed up and
              lacking in expression. Your ego is limp.
              You are becoming your own teacher.

Brown   You must face reality and allow life to
              move freely. You are becoming untangled
              in your life.

Life's Table Setting

Imagine before you a knife, fork and spoon. Now pick
up one of these utensils. Which one is it? Remember, use
the symbol or thought that comes to you first. The utensil
you chose will tell you how you choose to learn your
lessons in life.

Utensil: *Interpretation:*

Fork   Your lessons come hard. You have a ten-
                  dency to make things harder than they

have to be. Spiritually you have chosen your lessons to be difficult. This is not a life or time where you will merely exist.

Spoon   Your lessons come easy. You are spoon fed by the spiritual world. Things just happen to fall into your life. Your faith is extremely important to you. You must trust that you are protected in all ways of life.

Knife   Your lessons are to take things as they come. You are prone to overanalyze or direct.

Putting Your House in Order

All of us become bored at times, or we begin to feel as though we are standing still. During these times we need some direction to get back on course. In this exercise you will see exactly what you need to stimulate a "new you."

Close your eyes and see yourself walking from room to room in your home. You will choose to stop in one of the rooms for awhile. To which room does your higher self lead you? Does it show you the kitchen? The bathroom? The room you choose will tell you what you can do to stimulate you life.

Room: *Interpretation:*

Kitchen   You need to stir new interest. Create a new hobby. Look at new friendships. If in a dead end job, seek a new one. You must give your life a facelift." Get cooking."

Living Room   You need relaxation in your life. Start no-
               ticing how many things you try to cram
               into a short period of time. Set aside time
               every day to do nothing!

Bedroom   You need to put to rest the old and accept
               the new. Look ahead.

Bath/   You are in a cleansing period in your life.
Laundry   You may have some difficult choices to
Room   make.

Put It in Writing

This is a very simple exercise for ascertaining your
current state of mind. Close your eyes. You have a choice
between a pencil or pen. Which do you choose?

Pencil   You want to be able to erase what you have
               done or will do. Permanency scares you.
               Temporariness is a characteristic of this
               choice.

Pen   You feel everything you do is permanent.
               You need to become more aware of the
               moment and let go.

You may also want to use this exercise to ask about the
permanency of a relationship in which you may be involved, whether personal or business. When asking if the
relationship will last, if you see a pen, you can feel comfortable it will continue indefinitely. A pencil would signify it is temporary and can be erased. It is telling you at

the least that the relationship cannot last without some changes being made.

You may return to these exercises and repeat them at any time. You may wish to write down the details of what you visualized in these first four exercises and to begin a notebook of the symblols and interpretations that emerge as you progress through the exercises in this book.

CHAPTER 8

The Power of Symbols

Symbols . . . carry the ego-mind beyond its definitive and limited third dimension to the undreamed-of dimensions of the human soul. They supply humanity with meaning and meaningfulness that make life something worth living.

Eugene Pascal

Symbols are powerful messages. As you delve deeper into the symbolic world, you will find that symbols possess a potent energy force. They are multidimensional. They, in a sense, have a life of their own. Allow them to express themselves fully. They can awaken in you feelings of love, fear, ecstasy and heartbreak. They can rekindle old feelings and reinforce new ones. They elevate you to the highest levels of awareness. Symbols are the seeds of inspiration. Your internal symbols will open to you depths of awareness beyond your present comprehension.

When we ignore the panorama available to us through symbols, we live only a painting of life. We paint our self-portrait from our physical image and community expectations and withdraw into that portrait. Many people live their entire lives reflecting only this self-portrait of themselves. When we limit life to the conscious perception, ignoring the power of the symbols of the inner self, we miss the depth, the flavor, the color and texture of our full selves. Through the symbology of the higher self, we have a rich, full life of many dimensions offered to us. Why live in two dimensions only? If you identify yourself only by what your conscious self tells you that you are, you miss the power open to you and live a condensation of life.

Symbols are also given to us in dreams. While we may ignore the persistent knock of our higher self on a conscious plane, it nevertheless seeks to speak to us as we sleep. Dreams are symbolic images that give us a great deal of insight if we remain open to their messages. The techniques of this book go a step beyond dreams, in that we are able to ask any question at any time and receive an answer that is in tune with the flow of life.

A scene in a movie once illustrated the leap of awareness that occurs when we allow the higher self to direct us. It involved an experiment in solving the Rubik's Cube, the multicolored cube whose sides can be twisted and turned in an effort to align all squares of a single color together. A young man was given the puzzle to solve blindfolded. As this would involve mere chance, the teacher suggested it would take 1.35 trillion years to find the solution in this manner. Then the instructor had a young lady stand behind the blindfolded student and direct him. As he began to twist the cube in one direction or another, she directed him either "no" to each anticipated wrong move or "yes" to each correct move. The teacher informed the class that at the rate of one move per second the solution time was reduced from 1.35 trillion years to two minutes.

Although I cannot confirm the accuracy of those time estimates—and know that I've never solved a Rubik's Cube in two minutes even with both eyes open—the principle is sound and the analogy is appropriate. By letting your higher self see for you and direct you, you can reduce the necessary time and expand your power trillions of times. Your higher self is standing behind you, looking over your shoulder, waiting to provide the vision you need. Through the power of symbols you overcome your blindfold.

A paradox of life is that through turning inward we are able to expand to the limits of the cosmos. The great challenge before us is to take that leap.

CHAPTER 9

A Synchronized Universe

The collective unconscious is that set of building blocks
from which human reality is made.
It's as if there is this great reservoir outside of time and space,
patterns or energy—from which everything is
drawn or everything is made.
Reality consists of patterns made upon this gridwork,
and like a gigantic spiderweb, if you pluck one part
of that web, other parts of it respond.

Stephen Segaller, Merrill Berger

Internal symbols displayed on your range of consciousness by your higher self provide you with incredible knowledge. The focus of the exercises in this book is to give you all the skill you need in utilizing these symbols. In order to understand the scope of this phenomenon, it is helpful to look at the way internal symbols are complemented by the closely-related phenomenon of external symbols, which we encounter daily.

We live in a world of interrelationships. You and I are related to each other and to the rest of humanity to a degree which we do not yet comprehend. Similarly, our mental and physical worlds maintain a mysterious union, which mankind is only recently beginning to recognize.

We are not just clumps of matter maneuvering our way through the universe unconnected to others who are doing the same, looking only to avoid colliding with one another. We are each a part of a synchronized whole, with every part playing its role in the existence and movement of every other part. We are beginning to realize there is a magical blending of time and space and energy so that every thought and every movement impacts on every other thought and movement. Everything affects everything else. Every molecule has its place.

The direction of our thoughts and our actions sets off currents of energy which combine with and react to similar energy currents set in motion by other people and other events. The universe is a whole in which all forces impact upon each other. This interrelationship among all mental and physical elements of the universe often brings to the surface certain directional clues, which I categorize as external symbols. There are symbols occurring all around us that can provide meaningful guidance if we will be attentive to them and learn from them.

It is exciting to recognize the interplay of time and other forces of the world, a phenomenon referred to as "synchronicity" by Carl Jung and others. Edward Whitmont in *The Symbolic Quest* has said:

> Outer events quite beyond our conscious control seem to correspond to and give form to various fundamental unconscious trends that are striving toward expression. A psychological problem that is taking shape within may concurrently find its enactment symbolically or directly through corresponding external events.

Verena Kast dates the concept of synchronized thought as far back as Hippocrates around 300 B.C. She notes in *The Dynamics of Symbols* that certain philosophers and physicists through the ages have examined the relationship between the mental and material worlds, and that the concept of synchronicity has been offered as an explanation for the curious interaction between the mental and physical forces at work in the world.

At one of my seminars a participant told me that he had looked at his watch as we were approaching the lunch break and found that it had stopped at 9:21, almost three hours before. That happened to be the exact time to the minute that the seminar had begun that morning. It was no accident that this watch, which had kept perfect time for twenty-seven years, five months and twenty-seven days, suddenly stopped as this person began to draw on the timeless world of the inner self.

This "stopping of time" was a perfect symbol for what takes place when we reach beyond our linear perception and access the wisdom of the soul. Our five physical senses are not designed to give us information beyond what we call the present. Time is only an arbitrary way of slicing up our existence on this earth into manageable days, hours and minutes. We find that if we can measure time by a calendar and identify birthdays and other events, we can fasten into place some portion of our lives. The soul, however, travels free of any time table. The stopping of this watch, as we entered the realm of the soul in the seminar, reflected the absence of time as a relevant unit of measure to the higher self, for whom the past, present and future all coexist, interrelate and impact upon one another.

I have since found that this stopping of time has been documented from time to time in history. Carl Jung has written about this phenomenon in *Man and His Symbols:*

There are numerous well-authenticated stories of clocks stopping at the moment of their owner's death; one was the pendulum clock in the palace of Frederick the Great at Sans Souci, which stopped when the king died. Other common examples [of the cooperation of inanimate objects with the unconscious] are those of a mirror that breaks, or a picture that falls, when a death occurs; or minor but unexplained breakages in a house where someone is passing through an emotional crisis.

Synchronicity is one of the most intriguing aspects of life. Apparent coincidences are not coincidences at all. Relationships suddenly appear from seemingly random events. The connection was there all along; we were simply unable to recognize it. Haven't you thought of someone you haven't talked with for a long time and received a call from him almost immediately thereafter?

Everything is related in our world. What appears to be a coincidence is actually an inevitable positioning of energy forces. When you decide to take some action, your decision throws into gear various interlocking reactions. There is never a vacuum since all of life's gears form a perfect mesh.

Since there is no linear time outside our limited understanding, the ordering of events in chronological sequence is unnecessary. So we may "preview" an event in dream or thought and be shocked to see it unfold in "reality." On other occasions we are surprised at the timeliness of certain events that we assumed were unrelated.

I was told by a client of mine, who is a lawyer, about a surprising interconnection that could not be written off as coincidence. One morning he was researching a legal issue for an upcoming trial in his law library. He removed a casebook from the shelf and opened it to a case he hoped would be helpful on a question of constitutional law. Just as he turned to the proper page, he received a message that a new client was calling on the telephone. He took the call and learned that this person had a serious problem in a distant city, which would require locating a lawyer there.

Having agreed to help find a qualified attorney in that city, the lawyer hung up the telephone and returned to his research. When he again picked up the law book, the first name he saw was that of a lawyer friend of his (from law school days) located in the exact city in which he needed to find a lawyer! Although he had not seen or talked with this friend in thirty years, the man was exactly the person he needed. Therefore, my lawyer client had been opening the book to the page with the needed answer at the exact moment that someone else was dialing his number to ask the question!

This is indeed a synchronized universe. We are consciously unaware of the relationships of time, space and matter. We don't see the adjusting and readjusting that occurs as waves of energy are sent out to combine and interact with incoming waves. But we can marvel at the results. The more aware we become, the more we notice these synchronistic events that occur around us every day.

CHAPTER 10

Surrounded by Clues

Nature speaks in symbols and in signs.
John Greenleaf Whittier

Not only does the interaction of mental and physical forces produce effects in our lives that are both interesting and amusing, but it often produces meaningful external symbols that can provide a great deal of guidance if we will be alert to them.

A good principle to remember is that nothing happens by accident. By paying close attention to the signals around us, you can gain clues to the directions in which universal forces are moving. Opportunities open up to you at a particular time for a reason. Symbols give you clues to understanding when to act and when to wait. Symbols represent something. Often an external event can provide some direction as to an action that is either ripe or perhaps should be put on hold temporarily. Obedience to such symbols can mean the difference between going downstream with the flow of life and trying to paddle your canoe against a persistent current. It can also mean the difference between success and failure.

The symbols from your external life can tell you how to deal with life's relationships, where to look for the connecting links that can move you forward in this life of learning. They can tell you when to detour as well. Occurrences that may appear meaningless are actually telling you a great deal about yourself. A client was involved in a business partnership that had been a source of growth to her since she had worked hard to make the business a success. When she went into that business, a friend had given her a plant with a note saying she hoped the business would "blossom and grow as the plant does." Ultimately my client decided the business was draining her and that she would talk with her partner about getting out. On the very day she expected to talk with her partner, she found this plant dead. She had "accidentally" left it in the sun too long. Although she had many other plants that continued to thrive, this plant, which signified her business venture, was "burned out," just as she was.

Still another client was involved in a personal relationship that had run its course. Neither she nor her boyfriend was willing to admit their relationship had become a mere habit and that it was time for each of them to move ahead separately. One morning she awoke with the conviction that she could no longer delay the inevitable—that it was time to break off the romance. She glanced at the watch her boyfriend had given her several months before only to find that it had stopped during the night! Time had run out on this relationship. Can we say this was a coincidence? This is another illustration of the interaction of time, its physical manifestation, and other forces at work.

It is indeed fascinating to study the interrelationships of all of the earth's energies. One client, who was very anxious over problems that were developing in her life, contacted me for her first reading with a sense of great urgency in her voice. Due to an unexpected cancellation, I was able to shortcut the usual waiting period by several weeks (which undoubtedly was no accident either). Through the insight of the Guides we explored the upheavals in her business and social life. She was an executive in a large company and was being transferred to another city. She was being asked to uproot her home and all of the relationships she had developed over the course of twenty years. The thought of making this transition was devastating to her.

The Guides listened to her pour out her questions and anguish for an hour and responded from depths of awareness that she had never imagined. Her reading enabled her to gain a momentary perspective on her problem and to look at the move as a positive beginning. She left my office with a renewed attitude, even what might be described as enthusiasm.

She took with her the tape recording of her session. For a number of years I have made it a practice to record my readings, since the rush of information is usually too much for a person to absorb during the reading itself. Plus, it is often an emotional time of reuniting with other lives and souls, facing suppressed weaknesses and making new beginnings. So I give each client a cassette of the actual reading to be heard and digested later.

This young woman had a rare intensity about her. I later learned she played her tape on her drive to work each morning and again when she returned home at night. It became an integral part of her life. It was always with her. She discussed it with many of her friends.

Suddenly one day one of those friends answered this client's telephone call to find she was frantic to the point of hysteria. Her tape was blank! She had no idea how it could have been erased, since her tape player didn't even have

the capacity to erase a tape. Upon deeper reflection, however, the reason for the disappearance became clear: the
tape was becoming her God. Instead of drawing strength
from the knowledge it gave her, she had begun to use it as
a crutch. She was becoming addicted to it, so the Guides
erased it!

I have known this to happen on other occasions. Some
clients have found empty gaps to appear on their tapes
where their best interest lies in the removal of the message.
This may at times happen in a commonplace manner as
someone "accidentally" presses the wrong switch, but it is
no accident.

Such events demonstrate clearly the relationship between the internal and the external. Symbols in both
realms can provide us with direction. Whether internal or
external, symbols consist of a power that can make a vital
difference in your life. If you learn to pay attention to the
symbology that abounds in life, you no longer need to
walk blindly in your world.

ى

CHAPTER 11

Universal, Cultural and Personal Symbols

*Symbols are the sole language that can describe realities
that are not of a three-dimensional nature.*

Eugene Pascal

*It is the role of religious symbols to give a meaning
to the life of man.*

Carl G. Jung

Before journeying further into the exercises to develop
your symbolic vocabulary, it is helpful to understand that
symbols, individually or in groups, have many and varied
levels of meaning.

I have found it useful to divide the symbols that find
their way into the dialogue between a person and his
higher self into three categories. First, there are some
symbols which have a universal quality. They are a part of
common understanding among fellow travelers in this
and other lives. They transcend languages and cultures.
They often deal with enduring concepts of love, life and
death. The meaning of such symbols is woven into the
fabric of the symbol itself. For example, a hatching egg

represents a new beginning. A Chinese fisherman on the opposite side of the world would interpret a universal symbol as conveying the same message as you or I would.

Second, there are cultural symbols. These do not have the same eternal validity as universal symbols, but they do have cultural weight and significance. Symbols in this class extend to the boundaries of our cultural circles. These circles are both large and small as well as overlapping, depending upon whether they are defined by language, race, occupation, locale or some other aspect of our culture that unites us into groups. Our common experiences within these respective groups will give some symbols definition. Thus, within each cultural circle, symbols related to the focus of that circle will be uniform for each member of the circle. It is therefore possible for me to learn something about you from your relationship to these common symbols. For instance, in the North American culture, white signifies purity and is expected to be the predominant color of a young lady's wedding. In many Oriental cultures, on the other hand, weddings are splashed with the color red, whereas white symbolizes death. Our culture has taught us to think of the owl as signifying wisdom and the fox slyness.

The third category of symbols consists of personal symbols. These exist and arise out of your personal experiences in life and are unique to you. They do not necessarily hold the same meaning for anyone else. A symphony violinist might see a conductor's baton as representing a new direction, whereas a baton might have little or no symbolic relevance to someone unschooled in the music field. Lou Gehrig's number four could signify endurance to a baseball enthusiast, whereas Charles Lindbergh might mean the same thing to an aviator.

All three categories contribute to the vocabulary that will be used between you and your higher self. They all have equal validity for you.

As you move forward through the exercises in this book, you will be selecting symbols that feel appropriate to you to represent certain ideas or concepts. I have included at the back of the book an appendix of Common Symbols, which I have developed over the years. When no interpretation of your symbol comes readily to mind, you may wish to consult this appendix to see if the symbol listed there feels right to you. In many instances the symbols I use may be appropriate for your use as well, since they are the products of experiences, education and influences that we may have had in common. That is, many of these symbols fall into the universal and cultural categories. However, wherever you find that another symbol has a greater impact on you, this personal symbol is the one you should use.

Any time you feel a kinship between a certain image and an idea or interpretation, this is the symbol that conveys energy to you. This is the symbol that will propel strong and meaningful messages to your conscious mind. Although a particular symbol may fit 99% of the population, your unique experiences in life may cause a different image to be more appropriate. If so, that is the best symbol to use in communicating with your higher self. Other symbols may work, but the message will not be as clear. The best symbol for you is the one that produces the most precise message. There is a symbol that is right for you, whether it fits within the universal or cultural categories or arises out of your personal experience, and it has the perfect amount of built-in power to project a precise, penetrating meaning to you. Mark Twain, in speaking on the art of writing, said that the right word is as different from the almost-right word as lightning is from the lightning bug. So it is with symbols. Look for the lightning. Be attentive to the images that are most compelling to you.

After you have mastered communication through symbols, perhaps over a period of years, it is possible that you and your higher self will be so closely attuned that the messages will come automatically, without the use of the intermediate step of symbolism. This occurs with a blending of the conscious and the unconscious, which is a lofty aspiration. Until we reach that level of wholeness, whether in this life or a future existence, communication through symbols remains the most useful, meaningful way in which our conscious being can link up with our higher self and all the knowledge and awareness that it has to offer.

CHAPTER 12

A Matter of Time

We are symbols, and inhabit symbols.
Ralph Waldo Emerson

Time is invention or it is nothing at all.
Henri Bergson

Time is a means of measuring life on this earth. Units of time can also be useful in gaining insight for decisions important to your life. Over the years the Guides have given me a specific interpretation for each unit of time. In this way each hour of the day becomes symbolic of a precise attitude or expectation. This exercise is a direct and easy way to plug into guidance that can give you confidence in a correct decision or caution you concerning a questionable choice.

In Chapter One I asked you to visualize either a round-faced or digital clock and to note what time your clock was showing. If you have not pictured your clock already, focus on a clock of some kind. It may have the commanding presence of Big Ben or the delicate precision of a wristwatch. Next think of a question which you would like to have answered by your higher self.

Ask your question over and over in your mind, pushing everything else out of your thoughts. Then look to

44

8:31 pm

"your clock" for the answer. Your answer will come in the form of an actual time which can then be interpreted from the list provided below. Whether your time is A.M. or P.M. makes no difference.

INTERPRETATION: Perhaps you have asked the familiar question "Should I continue in my job?" If you saw the time 1:00 on your mental clock, you will find this suggests that "new beginnings" are at hand. Therefore, you can look forward to a likely change in employment. This answer suggests that you should be alert to new opportunities and gives you a basis for making new plans.

Not all responses will yield an exact hour. What if your clock reads 1:23 ? This simply means your response is more complex, and each number should be interpreted. The hour is the leading and dominant factor in your answer. The minutes expand on that premise, giving you a more detailed explanation. For example, in interpreting the time 1:23, you would interpret the hour 1:00 as a new beginning, encouraging a strong "go ahead." The 0:20 would offer a warning to maintain your balance by standing back and patiently letting things come your way. The 0:03 warns you not to become disorganized. It could also mean you will be called upon to use your creativity in some way. So in putting it all together, a new beginning lies ahead for you, but allow it to happen without forcing it. Also, make sure you stay balanced and focused by not allowing things to become scattered or disorganized.

If Your Clock Reads:	*Interpret It to Mean:*
1:00	A time to create new beginnings
2:00	Working on balance; using your intuitiion and sensitivity

3:00	Creating, organizing, expressing yourself or speaking out
4:00	Rolling up your sleeves and going to work; accepting struggle
5:00	A change is needed; paying attention to detail and striving for freedom
6:00	Feeling responsibility
7:00	Learning to think spiritually; a time to build confidence
8:00	Reaching your goals and enjoying success
9:00	A time to end; not a time for beginnings
10:00	Showing strength; blending, bonding
11:00	Taking immediate or sudden action
12:00	Making choices and decisions

In a world in which we have become so conscious of time and its demands upon us, it is appropriate to harness its energy in a way that gives us guidance. In the same way that early villagers measured their days by the courthouse clock in the square, your mental timepiece can direct you along your destiny's path.

CHAPTER 13

Techniques for Visualizing

Who we are is what we see and what we don't see.

Deena Metzger

Opening up to your inner self is something like the unfolding of a rosebud. Through symbology you receive knowledge and guidance that will unfold into a deeper and richer understanding of your life and the lives of those you love.

You will feel increasingly directed. Indeed, your life will gain direction and momentum, for you will be swimming with the current. You will connect with the God within, blending with that universal life force. You will never feel alone, for you will always be aware of the presence of your higher self.

Certain techniques will enable you to access more successfully the storehouse of knowledge available to you from your higher self. If you follow these steps, you will walk into a new level of awareness.

When seeking inner counsel, your mind should be clear and calm, without distractions. Also, as I have already suggested, whenever you are guided through these visualization exercises, it helps to see through the eyes of a child. Children have an openness about life and an excitement about new experiences that enhances their receptivity. This outlook often dims with adulthood, as caution and skepticism force aside trusting exuberance. Children also have an incredible gift of simplifying life, and that is one of the goals of inner communication practice. So try pretending that you are a child again as you progress through the guided daydreams in this program.

Finally, as you practice your inner communication skills, at times you may not receive a clear response or you may feel blocked. This is to be expected. There are times when even I find responses to be hazy. If this occurs, try taking a few deep breaths to raise your consciousness. Then rephrase your question and ask again. It is important to remember that your higher self wants to communicate with you as much as you want to communicate with it—perhaps more.

As you undertake these exercises, keep in mind that the goal of any process of communication with the higher self is to blend completely—to become one with the higher self. Recall the above techniques as you do the following exercise, and this will give you a clearer understanding of yourself.

Your Decorated Tree

There is much to be learned about your personality, your values, your interests and the way you deal with the world, from the vision of a decorated tree that rides in on the wave of your imagination. I think you will find this exercise to be both fun and enlightening.

Sit comfortably and take a few moments to relax your body and mind with a few deep breaths.

As you become more relaxed, picture a tree to be decorated by you for a special occasion, such as the New Year, Christmas or a wedding. You need not feel that you should draw on your recollection of past trees that you have decorated, but allow your imagination the freedom to express its creativity. As your tree comes into focus, notice all the details of the tree itself as well as any decorations it may display. Continue focusing on the details of your tree until you can give a complete and accurate description of it. If your thoughts begin to wander, gently bring your attention back to your tree.

When you have a complete description of your tree, open your eyes and answer the questions below. The details of your tree and its decorations can be interpreted to give you greater insight into yourself. Your decorated tree is simply a symbol for you—spiritually and emotionally.

Questions About Your Tree

Was the tree decorated?
If so, heavily or lightly?
Were the decorations distributed evenly? Or was there
    a skew toward the top or bottom half?
Were there lights on the tree?
If so, on or off?
One color or multiple colors?
Was there a decoration on the top of the tree?
Was the tree thick, sparse or about average?
What color was your tree?

INTERPRETATION: Decorations symbolize the degree to which you draw attention to yourself. Heavy decorations indicate that you are an extrovert who enjoys

attention. You stand out in a crowd, and people notice
you. You are very creative. Fewer decorations indicate
you dislike drawing attention to yourself and prefer to go
unnoticed in a crowd. You have a quiet nature. You guard
against being overwhelmed in life.

More decorations on the top half of your tree reveals
that you are extremely mental and intellectual. Your reactions are based on intellect rather than emotion. You look
beyond your day-to-day existence and needs. More decorations on the lower half indicates your inclination toward
the physical over the mental. You are dealing with the
physical aspects of life—money, health, business. Your
reactions in life are based more on black-and-white, yes-
and-no responses rather than an evaluation of the degrees
and nuances that may lie in between. Everything has to be
real in your mind. You are not one to go out on a limb for
something you cannot see, hear or feel. You are a true
"prove it" kind of person.

Antique ornaments on your tree indicate that you
value old things and that relationships with people are
long-lasting. You are a traditional type of person with
traditional values that have stood the test of time. Wooden
ornaments denote strength. If your ornaments happen to
be ragged and worn, you are tired, even exhausted, with
the people in your life. If your tree is loaded with ornaments, you probably still have your first doll or toy pistol.
You like to hold on. It is hard for you to clean out the closet.
You like all that clutter.

Bows on your tree mean you like attractive things, but
if the bows are plaid, this signifies confusion. Pink decorations reflect a very loving person. If you see money on
your tree, it may be a reflection of your material values.

Lights on a tree, if they are lighted, indicate the degree
to which you light up your world as well as the worlds of

others. If the lights are of different colors, you have many interests that keep you stimulated. If your lights are all one color, you are a more serene person who is more focused in your interest. The color of the lights may be telling you something as well. Red lights denote drama, intensity and even anger that may remain unresolved. You are a high-energy person.

A garland on a tree indicates you are keeping yourself somewhat confined. The garland wrapped around the tree parallels the confinements you have wrapped around yourself. Your world is orderly and always in place. Schedules are very important to you.

A decoration on top of your tree indicates that you are a goal-setter, one who is always reaching for the next level. You need a constant challenge. If there was no decoration on the top of your tree, you may not be motivating yourself enough. You need a "star" to reach for in order to grow.

The thickness of your tree reveals how "thick your skin is." A thick, bushy tree means you are tough as nails. You let very little affect you. Others see you as always in control and hard to get to know. You do not easily share your feelings. A sparse, thin tree means you are extremely sensitive. You are easily hurt because you are so "finely woven." You are an open book, and people feel they get to know you immediately.

What color was your tree? White represents spirituality. You are working on your spirituality now if you saw a white tree. A green tree symbolizes your physical being. It means you are at this time focused on the physical world.

A person in one of my workshops had a clear image of a cedar tree covered with dew. Since water denotes emotion, this would be a very emotional person. Since dew appears in the mornings, the particular emotion that is affecting this person is in the early stages. He has not gotten through the worst of it or the best of it, as the case may be.

What about artificial trees? If you visualized an artificial tree, you are concerned that you are not connecting with reality. You keep trying to prove to yourself over and over that you are real. Also, you may think you don't reveal your true self to others.

Your tree tells a great deal about you at this moment. The more insight you have into yourself, the better you are able to understand how daily events may affect you. The tree can help you learn how you tend to deal with the world. Such insights also give you direction in changing the attitudes with which you are not satisfied. Your tree reveals where you are right now. This of course can change if you wish.

Practicing this visualization exercise from time to time allows you to take a quick reading of your current state of consciousness. You can also use this technique to learn more about someone else, by visualizing his or her tree and its decorations.

CHAPTER 14

Developing Your Personal Symbology

In the depths of our being, beneath the layers of business
and buzzing confusion, is an ocean of creativity, wisdom
and joy which we can sometimes tap.
In its further reaches this ocean flows into
the endless sea of cosmic being.

Robert Ellwood

The ability to recognize and understand the messages your higher self is sending you can be developed easily. However, as with any talent or technique, a period of training and focus is required. The following series of exercises is a sort of spring training, a transition between the inactivity of the chilly months of nonawareness of the symbols in your life and the fulfillment of the summer season beyond in which your appreciation of symbology yields a fruitful harvest. In stretching your understanding and flexing your intuitiveness, you gain direction in listening to the messages of your higher self. Step-by-step you will become proficient in the fundamentals of communication with your higher self through symbology

EXERCISE #1: Relaxation and Concentration

> TIME: 5 minutes
> GOAL: To learn to relax the mind and body in order
>   to focus on receiving inner messages.

EXERCISE: With your eyes open, sit comfortably and relax. Feel each muscle in your face relaxing. Gently move your awareness downward into your neck and shoulder areas. When your upper body is completely relaxed, move on and feel the same relaxation in the rest of your body. Quickly scan these areas for tension. As you move down to your toes, become aware of how relaxed your whole body has become. Take a few minutes just to enjoy this calm and peaceful sensation before moving on to the next paragraph. Remember, the level of clarity from your inner guidance is in direct proportion to your level of relaxation and concentration.

You are now ready for a short exercise on concentration. First, read through the instructions in this paragraph. When you finish reading, close your eyes, take a few deep breaths and picture yourself walking down a path into a cool, green forest. Walk slowly, taking in all the sights, sounds and smells. Look at the sturdy trunks of the trees and the overhanging limbs sheltering your way. Listen to the breeze as it whispers among the leaves overhead. Smell the drifting fragrance of wildflowers. As you wind your way through this green forest, notice the animals you find there. Count as many different animals as you can see. You will surely see a rabbit darting through the underbrush. There will be squirrels jumping from limb to limb in a precarious game of chase. Look in every direction and take note of each animal you see.

Then count the different birds you see building nests, testing young wings and twittering their bird chatter. Keep a running count of all the animals and birds you see on your walk. This exercise opens the corridors of your imagination and dissolves any feeling of being scattered.

You are now ready to move forward to Exercise # 2.

EXERCISE #2: Developing the Inner Senses

TIME: 5 minutes
GOAL: To develop your inner senses.

EXERCISE: As you pull back the curtain to allow your higher self to speak to you, this communication will be in symbols. But as you develop your ability to receive these symbols, they will be less and less like the blackboard diagram of an elementary school teacher and more and more in the nature of living illustrations, appealing to all of your senses. It is helpful to orient your mind to receiving these multi-sensual signals.

Read each of the following phrases one at a time and close your eyes and experience the sense brought to mind by that phrase. A flash of insight will appear, and you will experience vividly the sense of sight, hearing, touch, smell or taste involved. If you are slow to grasp a particular image, simply move on to the next one. Do not linger on any one item. Just become aware of your senses. Your reactions will become stronger and sharper the more you practice this technique.

(1) *Sense the sight of . . .*

the face of a childhood teacher
a wallet full of money

the car that you drive
children on a playground
the face of your father
the room where you sleep
the glow of a candle

(2) *Sense the feel of* . . .

a hot shower
a cold shower
a relaxing massage
a new pair of shoes
the embrace of an old friend
a punch in the gut
a shampoo at the hairstylist's

(3) *Sense the smell of* . . .

the interior of a new car
a new baby
the baking of an apple pie
a cedar closet
Thanksgiving dinner
a campfire
your favorite cologne
a freshly-cut lawn

(4) *Sense the taste of* . . .

cranberry juice
an orange
a lemon
a cold glass of water
honey

your favorite dessert
a sour pickle
peppermint

(5) Sense the sound of . . .

a train passing nearby
an angry dog
a baby crying
your favorite song
a drum solo
a thunderstorm
a door slamming

The preceding exercise helps you to become familiar with your own imagination. You should go with your first impulse each time, the first thought that pops into your mind. Sometimes we receive some surprises. When you were thinking of the face of a childhood teacher, you might have been surprised to see a high school or college teacher appear. This may reflect your perception of your development at that point. Or, when asked to picture the room where you sleep, your room of thirty years ago might suddenly be surrounding you. You begin to realize that you are not entirely in control of these images. Your higher self is directing the dialogue. Be alert for the unusual symbol. It could have significance for you.

This exercise will have stimulated your imagination and your receptive powers.

EXERCISE # 3: Communication Symbols

TIME: 20-30 minutes
GOAL: To begin identifying the symbols that your inner self will use to communicate with you.

EXERCISE: You are sweeping away the dust from mental hallways that have remained untraveled for years. We have traditionally thought of our imagination as a diversion from real life. It has been the stuff of idle daydreams of childhood. It is an activity that most of us were taught to outgrow, and we have sought to do just that.

In doing so we have been suppressing the greatest source of knowledge and insight available to us in this life. The ability to reach deep inside and contact the inner self opens resources to us that we can never find in the physical world. This exercise further enhances that connection.

One by one, read the following words and phrases and notice the first picture that comes to mind. Describe the picture using words or drawings next to the word itself. Your descriptions or illustrations should be as simple as possible. If nothing comes to mind, move on to the next word and come back later to the ones on which you hesitated. The picture you receive is the symbol your inner self will use to communicate that idea to you. You should record your first instinctive response to each phrase, but be flexible in changing your symbol at a later time if you feel strongly about a different image that comes to mind. You may also wish to add some phrases of your own to this list in order to expand your vocabulary with your inner guidance.

This exercise should be repeated as often as possible in order to strengthen your symbols. The more you practice, the stronger your symbols will become. This in turn will strengthen your inner messages. Let go of the ego and you will excel at receiving answers from within. Your list of symbols should be maintained and updated as you repeat this exercise in the future. This is your personalized symbol dictionary.

EXAMPLES: Thinking of the phrase "confused" might suggest an image of a wrinkled forehead. "Slow in coming to fruition" might stir up the symbol of a snail.

Word or Phrase: *My Symbol:*

broken heart
change in home
procrastination
intuitive
hearing difficulty
communication
fearful
disappointment
overwhelmed
confident
impatient
hard-headed
musical
learning disability
talks too much
time alone needed
won't let go of the past
angry
lazy
moves slowly
writing ability
nurturing
mental confusion
secretive
compromise
mechanically inclined
blocked

leader
follower
new learning
scattered
sharp tongue
judgmental
negative
travel opportunity
jumps from one thing to another
distance needed
money
larger than life
recognition shown
exposed
hidden
intelligent
flexibility
movement
soft-hearted
expansion

Your completed list may look in part something like this, which I have filled in with symbols I use.

Word or Phrase: *My Symbol:*

broken heart   heart split in middle
change in home   boxes for packing
procrastination   snail
intuitive   crystal ball
discipline needed   switch
hearing difficulty   hands over ears
communication   telephone
fearful   hair standing up on head

disappointment   sad face
overwhelmed   waves in ocean washing
                        over head

EXERCISE #4: The Television and Famous Faces

TIME: 5 minutes
GOAL: To practice basic questions that you may
       wish to ask of your higher self.

EXERCISE: Our individual lives are dramas in which
we are the stars. Each of us is the featured performer in a
personal drama that is unlike anyone else's. We have each
had our share of ecstasy, heartbreak, work and play. Each
event of each day has combined to make us what we are
today. Our personalities, our aspirations and our needs
have shifted back and forth as the tides of each day have
washed over our lives and then receded, leaving us a little
different from the day before.

Yet we usually fail to have a clear perception of who
we are at any given time. Our higher self, unaffected by
the fog of insecurity and fear, has a sharp perception of
where life has taken us. It is exciting and enlightening to
have this secret revealed to us consciously as well.

The following questions will help to open to you an
understanding of how you look at the world and yourself
today. As you come to each question, close your eyes,
focus on that question and wait for the answer to come to
you. Accept the first image you receive without passing
judgment on it in any way. You can then interpret the
meaning of your answers by analyzing what those symbols mean to you.

If you believe a certain image came to mind because
someone had just mentioned it or you just saw a similar

image on television, let that image drift away and ask for the true image to come forward. Follow your instincts as to which images are pertinent. Be cautious of wanting a different symbol simply because you do not like the first one. Your symbols will change over time as your attitudes and states of consciousness change.

QUESTION 1: Picture a television set and then ask yourself, "What is playing on my television set?"

INTERPRETATION: This question allows your higher self to reveal to you how you are seeing the outside world at this time. Take time now to analyze the scene you saw on your television set. If you saw a love scene, you see the outside world as romantic, gentle and good. Life is carefree for you, and you generally go through life with a smile. If you saw a western, on the other hand, you see the world as somewhat threatening. You must always be ready to defend yourself. At any moment someone could ambush you from behind. If you saw a news show or a documentary, you view the world today as black and white. It is a yes or no kind of place and very intense. Things have to make sense to you. You may over-think situations.

A comedy reflects your view of today as being entertaining and funny. You are enjoying your life. You could go to an airport and enjoy just watching the people coming and going. You are not one to become ruffled. Others enjoy being around you. If you saw a sports program, you see life at this time as a game in which someone always wins and someone always loses. You are very competitive. A stock broker or a lawyer might have this perception, for example.

If you found yourself watching a sitcom, your life is having some ups and downs but everything works out all right in the end. Your attitude is "life goes on."

This exercise should give you a valuable insight into the way you view your world today. You may be reassured to know that you feel O.K. about this existence. Or you may have found reason to make a concerted effort to improve your picture of your world.

QUESTION 2: What famous face best suits me?

INTERPRETATION: This question should provoke some interesting and valuable insight. As you visualize the face of a famous person that best suits you, you are receiving an indication of how your higher self sees you. It is similar to feedback concerning the impression you make on a job interview or a first date—except that your higher self knows you better than you may wish to admit. Therefore, this is a very revealing question.

After you have received the image, ask yourself what that person symbolizes or means to you. Do not base your interpretation on what someone else may believe about this person. This is personal to you. You will learn how your higher self sees you at this particular time in your life.

People in my workshops are often surprised by the images they receive. Our conscious self-image is often very different from the person we truly are inside. We have the ability to piece together an artificial image of ourselves that may be brave and debonair in contrast to the uncertainties that we keep buried within. There are those who have never allowed the qualities of caring and love to escape a protective exterior. This question is designed to pull a vision of who you actually are from a deeper part of you.

If you saw Abraham Lincoln, what message does that send to you? Lincoln is known for being honest as well as self-educated. We see his solemn face erect and committed in the face of tremendous problems. He stands tall while the storm rages all around him. Your higher self would be seeing you as dependable and dedicated. You are seen as strong and compassionate, even in the face of criticism.

Lucille Ball is, of course, known for being one of the great comediennes of our time. She is also known as a very strong-willed woman with a drive to succeed. She had a great deal of inner strength with an external overlay of playing the clown. She was always able to laugh at herself. If you saw her, your higher self ascribes these characteristics to you. Usually when someone sees a movie star in this exercise, there is a theatrical aspect to his life. Things have to happen in a big way for this person. Sometimes subtleties go over his head.

How do you see George Washington? If your perception of him is rooted in your early years, you probably view him as a leader who endured the icy chill of crossing the Delaware and an honest son who would not lie about the cherry tree. Indeed, most of us spent the fourth grade looking at the painting of Washington hanging over the classroom blackboard. It conveyed the essence of calm stability. If your focus developed as an adult, you may see Washington as a wealthy landowner with a home overlooking a scenic bend in the Potomac. You may also see him as the self-sacrificing statesman who was willing to leave a life of luxury to serve the people of this country.

Many in my workshops see sports stars. Unless there is a personal characteristic of the individual that stands out, such an image connotes the obvious attributes of aggressiveness and strength of will. An athlete is a competitor, willing to risk failure for the chance of victory. If you visualized a sports star, your higher self probably sees you as one who is able to take charge and likes a challenge.

Other people see political figures. Some see John F. Kennedy, others Richard Nixon. Obviously these images have different meanings for different people. A political figure may represent a positive or a negative image depending upon your own perception of him.

You may see a different face next week or next month from the one you saw today. These display different aspects of your nature. They may also reflect a change in your life.

It is always interesting in my workshops to find that a large percentage of people are presented images of famous people that they never would have chosen consciously. When they consider it, they find that the image fits. Yet they insist they would have selected someone else if given time to analyze the question through their conscious minds.

The images you receive in this exercise emerge from a symbolic level, even a spiritual level. They transcend the emotional and intellectual plateaus. You may be pleasantly surprised or chagrined, but greater knowledge of your real self-image provides greater potential for growth.

CHAPTER 15

Trusting Your Intuition

The seat of the soul is there
where the inner and outer worlds meet.

Novalis

Over the past few years, I have given many workshops teaching the principles in this book. The most common question from workshop participants is, "How do I know if it's my higher self communicating with me rather than my just making up what I want to hear?" You must trust your intuition. This is perhaps the biggest hurdle to overcome when you start on the path of communicating with your higher self. It is common to believe that you are simply "making it up" because the only tool available to your inner guidance is your conscious mind. It is natural and expected for one to question the validity of these messages. Release the fear of being wrong, and you will be a success in communicating with your higher self.

Another tip that will help you recognize that you are not just "making it up" is to look for an unusual symbol or image. If the image you receive is not one that would ordinarily be a part of your thoughts or speech, this reinforces the knowledge that it is coming to you from someplace else—your higher self. A person considering a new business venture saw a camel, which signaled that the venture would take great endurance. The idea of a camel was totally foreign to this person's daily experiences and conscious thought. He could not recall any context in which he had thought of a camel for years. This underscored the validity of the camel as a symbol transmitted from another level of consciousness.

One client asked her higher self for a sign regarding a former boyfriend for whom she still had strong feelings. She was considering resuming the relationship. The first sign she received was a geometry compass, something she had not seen or used since her geometry class in high school. It was indeed an unusual symbol, so she recalled how a compass is used. She concluded that the relationship had come full circle (a term they had, in fact, used in their discussions). Also, she realized that there was no point in retracing the same circle. Hopeful that she might have misinterpreted this symbol, she asked for another for clarification. Almost immediately she saw a tombstone. The romance was dead.

With some questions your signs may be very clear. For instance, you may wonder about a proposed business venture. In asking your inner guidance whether or not a certain idea would be a financially sound and rewarding experience for you, you are shown a stop sign. That one is obvious. Your inner guidance is suggesting that this is not a proposal on which to go forward. Perhaps the symbol is a snail, indicating that the business venture will be slow in coming to fruition or move along at a snail's pace.

You will learn to trust your intuition with practice and with testing the advice that you are given over time. Listen to your gut feelings and honestly appraise the messages you are receiving. You will reach a point when you can no longer deny the accuracy of your own inner guidance. The very root of your existence knows you better than you consciously know yourself. You can trust the fact that this core, your higher self, always has your best interests at heart. Your higher self is here to help you, to encourage you, to provide you with strength and guidance. You must trust that the teachings you receive are pure and gain confidence in your intuition.

CHAPTER 16

Focusing Your Questions

Of all the kinds of joy, none perhaps is so pure
as that occasioned by sudden insight.

Robert Grudin

How can you insure that the images that are flashed before you are the symbols that are most meaningful to you? One way is to frame your questions as clearly and precisely as possible. You will receive clear and direct answers in proportion to the clarity and directness with which you ask your questions.

This technique opens the book of knowledge to the right chapter by focusing your thinking. Fuzzy thinking is one of the obstacles to a command of life today. Our feet take us in one direction while our mind wanders in another. Too often we fail to identify exactly what we want and expect from life. Without a destination we are prone to meander aimlessly through life. Proper focus helps to align all our energies into the same direction. This helps to promote a clear response from your higher self.

Assume that you are having some problems in your marriage. You want to work things out but are uncertain how to do it. You might ask your higher self, "Tell me about my marriage." This request might yield a cloud, meaning that you are feeling confusion over the marriage.

69

But you already knew that. What you want is guidance, something that can help you move forward.

It would be better to ask, "Is there anything I can do to help solve the problems in my marriage?" This is a more direct way to seek what you really want. This clearly worded question might give you an image of a bouncing ball, indicating that greater flexibility on your part would alleviate some of the problems.

You may think the wording is not important and that your higher self will know what you really want to know. Your inner guidance will guide you based only on what you clearly ask. The storehouse of knowledge is available to you, but you must ask the question. If you go into a library for information on the origin of the Mona Lisa, the librarian does not meet you at the door with a stack of references on the painting and the artist, Leonardo da Vinci. The information is available, but you must initiate the inquiry. Similarly, television offers us a wide selection of information and entertainment. But to gain access to a particular program we must make the connection by dialing the desired channel.

In the same manner, tap into the current of your higher self by asking a clear, direct question. Don't ask, "What should I do about my work?" Ask instead, "How can I become a better counselor?" Or "How can I improve my relationship with my boss?" Or "How can I increase sales in my territory?" Your higher self will tell you. If the symbol received is not clear to you, simply ask for another symbol. If you get nothing more or the new symbol is still not clear, perhaps you need to revise your question.

Gain sharp insight by asking clear and precise questions. Focus as to your questioning and focus as to the direction you are moving through life go hand in hand. Communication with your higher self is not an isolated activity. It is interrelated with the rest of your being. As you strengthen and define your attitudes in life, you strengthen your communication skills. Your mental, physical and spiritual existences, your internal and external worlds, all combine to form a total life. All work together to allow you to grow as a person. With the ability to focus precisely, you raise inner communication to its most effective and exciting level.

CHAPTER 17

Relaxing into a "Receiving Mode"

Divine truth is an endless ocean,
with cresting waves and still depths.

Robert Ellwood

Becoming centered through relaxation is important to opening the channel of inner communication. Being centered means setting aside a few moments alone to relax— in a quiet, peaceful place, where you know you will not be interrupted. It is important to relax both the body and the mind in order to open a clear channel for your inner God.

Unfortunately, life in today's fast-paced world does not allow for very much relaxation. The transition from business meetings, car pooling and other tensions of a normal day to a state of serene relaxation does not come automatically. It often helps to have a specific exercise available to make this shift from hurricane to summer breeze.

The following exercise provides some helpful relaxation techniques. Sit in a quiet place and focus on relaxing your body. As you read through this exercise, become mentally aware of everything within you. Notice how your body feels. Notice your thoughts. Take a few deep breaths and be aware of your breathing as you do. As you inhale, feel yourself pulling the air from your toes, through your entire body, and all the way to the top of your head. As you exhale, allow your body to go completely limp, pushing all the air out. Notice that each time you take a deep breath, you become still more focused.

As you finish your last deep breath, mentally picture a peaceful, tranquil meadow. Notice all the visual details of your meadow. Notice the trees gently swaying in the wind. Feel the movement of the breeze around you, lightly blowing your hair. Smell the air. It smells sweet and fresh and alive. Notice the sounds of the animals in your meadow. You hear the birds and squirrels, and you look around to see if you can see them. Their sounds are so familiar that you're sure you must know the animals well.

Imagine what it would be like to live here in this quiet spot forever. Take a few minutes just to look around and become one with the feelings of your meadow. Let yourself leave your physical body and simply blend with the meadow. Notice how still and alive you feel. You are completely at peace. All tensions have disappeared. You feel revitalized and aware of your body once more. Take a few deep breaths and stretch.

This should put you into an ideal frame of mind for receiving clear symbols. You can alternate this scene with other images that give you a feeling of calmness. It might be a white, sandy beach with warm waves lapping up onto the shore in a slow rhythm. Or you might picture a cool forest in which the breeze whispers through the treetops and the autumn leaves make their slow descent to the earth.

At other times you may become centered merely by repeating the word "calm" to yourself over and over. Whatever naturally induces relaxation for you is helpful. I include the word "natural" because drugs and alcohol, while perhaps relaxing, actually inhibit communication. They block your ability to receive and recall communication from your higher self.

Some people find that if they meditate for a short period of time before seeking inner guidance, they receive stronger messages. Meditation is not imperative, however. Do whatever works best for you. Eliminating the distractions that bombard the senses and achieving a peaceful relaxation of mind and body opens the passageway to higher knowledge.

CHAPTER 18

Strengthening Your Inner Awareness

As a plant produces its flower,
so the psyche creates its symbols.

Carl G. Jung

At this point I hope that you are becoming comfortable in the knowledge that communication with your intuitive self is not only possible but a valuable resource available to you at all times. The next exercises will continue to strengthen your inner awareness. Through repetition you will become able to plug into your higher energy source much like switching on the lights in your living room.

EXERCISE: #1: A Rose Is a Rose

TIME: 5 minutes

GOAL: To strengthen the ability to recall visualization details.

EXERCISE: Close your eyes and see before you a closed rosebud. Closely examine all the details of this mental image. Notice the texture of the bud. See the beads of moisture standing on the bud. Watch as the bud slowly—very slowly—opens. Watch until it is completely opened. Now look into the opened rose. Smell its sweet aroma. Softly touch the petals and notice how they feel. Are they soft? Wet? Now remove the rose from your vision completely and open your eyes.

Write down everything you remember about the rose in your journal. What fragrance did you smell? How quickly did it open? What color was it? Could you really see the moisture on the rose? Describe the feelings you experienced about the rose. How did you feel when the rose opened? Did you feel excited or bored?

This exercise may seem rather mundane. However, this type of practice strengthens your ability to gain clarity in your higher self communications. More important, it teaches how to see value and depth in everything about your life, no matter how insignificant it may initially appear. EVERYTHING is important.

EXERCISE #2: Interpreting Symbols

TIME: 5 minutes
GOAL: To learn to interpret symbols as you receive them.

EXERCISE: Read each of the following symbols one at a time. As you mentally picture each symbol, ask yourself, "What does this image mean to me?" Then record your first response next to each symbol listed. Two people may have entirely different interpretations of the same symbol. Your higher self knows how you will interpret different images and will therefore send the appropriate one to you. This type of exercise will help you build a more extensive vocabulary with which to communicate with your inner guidance.

You may wish to compare your interpretations with those in the symbol appendix at the back of this book when you have completed the exercise. If your interpretations do not match those offered in the appendix, this does not matter. It is your personal response that has meaning for you.

EXAMPLE: Seeing an "anchor" brings to mind stability, holding still or holding in place.

Symbol: *My Interpretation or Definition:*

horn
wall
kangaroo
patio
arrow
frog
guitar
luggage
whip
star
telephone
hands reaching out
razor
alligator
robot
flower
praying hands
glove
rope
amusement park
kite

EXERCISE #3: It's in the Palm of Your Hand

TIME: 5 minutes
GOAL: To practice requesting and receiving general
           guidance.

EXERCISE: Close your eyes, take a few deep breaths, and ask your higher self to provide you with insight. Have confidence that what will be given to you is of value. Then see before you your open hand with the palm turned upward. Tightly squeeze your hand into a fist. Then slowly open the fist, knowing that the answer will be there. What is in the palm of your hand? Do you recall trying this exercise in Chapter Two? Did you see different objects then and now?

Your fist represents a holding on, and whatever you visualized in your hand is something you are holding onto or which is causing a retarding of progress. One client pictured a chicken. She recognized this as being symbolic of something about which she felt cowardly or which she was afraid to face. This exercise called that situation to the forefront and helped her to confront it. A rope in your palm would indicate that you are feeling tied down to a relationship, a job or some other area of life.

If you pictured a handful of random little objects, this illustrates clutter in your life that should be discarded. A broom would suggest that you are holding onto something that should be swept aside. This could be an attitude or a relationship with someone. A stack of money or other valuables could indicate that an overly materialistic attitude is slowing your spiritual growth.

This exercise is fun and simple to perform on a regular basis. You may be surprised at what you are shown. The objects usually change from time to time.

EXERCISE #4: Awareness Techniques

TIME: 10 minutes

GOAL: To develop awareness techniques to understand better the nature of self and others.

EXERCISE: Take a moment to become centered. Then
close your eyes and ask your inner God for assistance in
picturing an animal that best describes you. Wait for the
image to appear, trusting in your intuitive side for appropriate and meaningful responses. Remind yourself there
are no right or wrong answers. When your symbol is clear,
open your eyes and write down the type of animal you
have seen.

Now ask yourself, "What does this animal mean to
me? What does it represent to me?" Is it wild? Domesti-
cated? Slow? Fast? Dangerous? Obedient?

There are many animals your higher self could draw
from to paint a portrait of you. What has this particular
animal told you by its selection? This exercise offers wonderful insight into the type of person you are. It also
strengthens your ability to "see."

You may want to take this exercise a step further by
applying the animal symbol to other people in your life—
friends, family, co-workers or any other person who is
important to your world. Focus on one person at a time,
and wait for a response from your higher self. You may
find it easier to match animals with other people than with
yourself. Where other people are concerned, it may be
helpful to ask yourself whether the animal received fright-
ens you or makes you feel secure. This will help you
understand the temperament of each such person at his
very core and how that relates to your life.

EXAMPLES: If you receive a tiger, it may indicate that you like to roam around and are difficult to pin down to any particular thing. You are hard to catch, have a lot of energy and love adventure. If you receive a bear, I would interpret that as being lovable and cuddly like a teddy bear. A bird would indicate a desire to be free. A dog with a wagging tail would suggest a playful, entertaining nature. That same dog showing his teeth would reflect an angry, defensive person. A cat is intuitive. It has nine lives. You usually land on your feet no matter how long the fall.

If you are applying this exercise to another person in your life, there are several obvious animals that require caution. A shark or an alligator will eat you alive and is not to be trusted. You will often feel drained around this person. A fox is typically sly. A whale will give you a feeling of being overwhelmed.

EXERCISE #5: Expanding the Vocabulary

TIME: 10 minutes
GOAL: To practice receiving more symbols.

EXERCISE: Read each of the following words or phrases to yourself, one at a time. After each one, close your eyes and focus on that particular word until an image comes into your thoughts. Then open your eyes and write down the word and the correlating symbol. If nothing comes to mind for a particular word, simply move on and try that word again another day.

What do you see when describing someone who is:

handicapped
brilliant

confined
tired
sick
scattered
worried
negative
talkative
confused
shy

Now think of twenty or so different descriptive terms, phrases or signs you would like to develop with your inner guidance. Then take them one at a time and ask for the correlating symbol. You will build a strong personalized dictionary of symbology in no time.

EXERCISE #6: Inner Emotions

TIME: 5 minutes
GOAL: To learn to feel a variety of inner emotions
to strengthen communication.

EXERCISE: Take a minute to quiet your mind. Read each of the following sensations one at a time. Then close your eyes and experience the corresponding emotion. By understanding and interpreting your emotional responses, you will gain greater clarity from your inner guidance. Sometimes a symbol alone does not communicate the full message. However, when that symbol is coupled with an emotional response, the message becomes increasingly clear. Just go with the feeling as it comes to you. This exercise helps you to add another dimension to the symbols you are using. It gives depth to each experience.

Feel the emotion of:

the smell of fresh cider
an auditorium full of applause for you
a painful toothache
the joy of a new day
seeing an old friend
seeing your mother
being alone and lonely
flying in a small aircraft
a warm, friendly handshake
the sudden death of a loved one
breaking free from confinement
your first kiss
a thunder and lightning storm
having a baby
a job well done
the first day of vacation
Christmas as a child
getting hired for your first job
being the last child picked for kickball
breaking off a relationship
achieving a huge victory

Just as a picture is worth a thousand words, a picture complete with the sounds, smells and feeling of an experience multiplies the impact of that picture in richness and meaning.

CHAPTER 19

Blending the Inner and Outer Dimensions

*One after another the greatest writers, poets, and artists
confirm the fact that their work comes to them
from beyond the threshold of consciousness.*

Shelley

In the preceding exercises you have utilized a variety
of techniques that helped you to quiet your mind, focus,
and become comfortable with receiving and interpreting
symbols. You have begun to listen to your inner voice. It is
at this time that you are most able to experience life—or
any challenging situation—with clarity and calm.

How then can you create a consistent pattern of still-
ness within your life? First, you must confront any addictions in your life that might be distracting you from experiencing your inner self. In other words, examine those
patterns of repeated behavior from which the necessary
lessons were never appreciated or acknowledged. How
many times have you closed a problem door in your life
only to open it again? How many times have you felt
lonely and not recognized the importance of that time
alone? You need to become focused in the present mo
ment in life and become addicted to living life fully.

You should be conscious of giving adequate attention to the spiritual realm of who you are. In doing so, the physical dimension will reap the benefits as well. It is important to devote attention to your concentration and imagination. This promotes a blending of your physical and spiritual dimensions, permitting you to achieve a more powerful and fulfilling life. Communicating with your inner God allows you to tap into and unfold that spiritual dimension which can then blend with the physical.

Your concentration is scattered when you find there is too little time alone for you and your inner God. This leads to frustration and spiritual paralysis. Taking the time to blend the physical and spiritual breaks this paralysis and gives you power. You receive a new level of guidance and an awareness of the power that is yours. More important, you own your power, and thus you own your life. Blending your physical and spiritual dimensions allows you to cast aside addictions and to live life fully in the moment.

EXERCISE #1: Connecting with the Winds of Destiny

TIME: 10 minutes
GOAL: To become comfortable owning your power.

EXERCISE: Find a comfortable place to be still and close your eyes. Stretch out and relax your entire body.

Imagine yourself as a child in a windstorm. Feel the wind as it gusts around you. You are having difficulty just standing still. You are being pushed and pulled in many different directions. The wind is blowing in your eyes and you cannot see anything. You cannot hear anything but the howl of the wind. You have no idea where you are or what you can do to get out of the storm. The more the wind blows, the more alone and frightened you feel. You are frustrated and desperate.

The only way to safety is to pull hard against the wind and take control of your total being. You immediately apply every ounce of strength you have against the wind. As you do, the wind suddenly becomes still. You are amazed that the wind becomes quiet once you make the decision to apply yourself. All you have to do is concentrate and take control. Connect with your inner self. When you connect, the wind stops and you are in control.

Now open your eyes and know that whenever you find yourself in one of life's windstorms, you need only to concentrate and take control in order to calm the winds. There is no need to be scattered about by the winds of fear and frustration. They will come, but when they hit, rest assured you have the inner strength and guidance to subdue them. They, too, shall pass.

EXERCISE #2: Getting to Know You

    TIME: 10 minutes

    GOAL: To communicate with your higher self to
                 understand better other people in your life.

EXERCISE: List ten people in your life whom you know well. Be sure to leave space next to each name so that you can record a symbol there.

When your list is complete, take each name and focus on it. At the same time, ask your higher self for a symbol that describes this person. When you receive the symbol, open your eyes and write it next to the name. As before, take the first thought or symbol you receive. The symbol should flow into your consciousness quickly and easily. If there is any hesitation, move on to the next name and return to the blocked name when you have finished the others. If you are still having difficulty, take three deep breaths and try once more. After you have completed the entire exercise, analyze what each of these symbols means to you. See what insight these symbols give you about those names you have listed.

Next, make a list of five people whom you would like to know better. These can be co-workers, friends of friends, or anyone else accessible to you. Again, focus on each name and ask your higher self for a symbol that best describes that person. Write down your responses. Then review these symbols and their meanings.

Then take the next step. Go through each name on your list of five and ask your higher self for a symbol that would help you get to know that person better. This may be more difficult, so don't get discouraged if the symbols are not clear. The more you work with your higher self, the more familiar you will become with your common language.

Now that you have completed the exercise, go back over each symbol and see if you agree with the responses your higher self offered. I promise you there will be some symbols you would not have come up with alone. Some symbols may be confusing to you at this time. If this is the case, simply record these and set them aside. They will make sense to you at a later time. It is not important that you understand everything that is given at this point. You and your higher self are just beginning to learn how to communicate with one another.

EXAMPLES:

Name:	Symbol:	Interpretation:
Bill	kangaroo	He jumps from one thing to another.
Joe	swan	He is graceful and always a gentleman.
Alice	hammer	She is very judgmental or tough as nails.
Sally	salt & pepper	She adds spice to your life.
Tom	horse	He has great strength.
Edna	flower	She makes you bloom and open to new aspects of life.

Remember, there are no coincidences, and everything is timed to perfection. Therefore, your reading this book is an indication you are ready to awaken that part of you that you might not have realized existed. It has simply been hibernating until the springtime of your awareness awakened it. You are actually more awake within yourself today than you have ever been.

CHAPTER 20

Mastering Your New Skills

The great masterpieces in art and in nature,
and the greatest masterpiece of all, Man, can be grasped
not by the brain but by the soul, the self—the intuitive *self.*
Henry Thomas, Dana Lee Thomas

You have now learned all you need to know about creating a dialogue with your higher self. From this point forward, it is simply a matter of practicing that dialogue, of sourcing your inner God for guidance and wisdom. The focus of the following exercises will be the exploration of a variety of formats for requesting guidance from your higher self.

EXERCISE #1: Higher Self Dialogue

TIME: 20 minutes
GOAL: To experiment with a variety of question
formats for your higher self.

EXERCISE: In this exercise you are to practice communicating with your higher self with certain questions that are significant to your life. The purpose is to see that there are many ways to seek guidance and insight from within and much valuable information to be gleaned from that guidance. From these examples you will learn to let your imagination be your guide in coming up with new and different questions. Close your eyes and take a moment to become centered before asking each question one at a time. When you receive an answer, you may want to write it down or just make a mental note of it. As your communication skills improve, you may receive several symbols. Simply write them down and keep asking if this is the last one. You will know when there are no more symbols coming for a particular question. The symbols build on one another.

When all your questions have been asked and answered, take some time to review and interpret your answers. In interpreting your symbols, it helps to ask yourself, "What does this symbol mean to me? What are the feelings I associate with this symbol?" These two questions will help you more clearly interpret the message from your higher self.

Questions To Be Asked of Your Higher Self:

(1) What year was a major turning point in my spirituality?

Your higher self will project a year onto your mental screen. After receiving your answer, think back to what was taking place in your life at that time. Examine your answer closely to understand what is being offered to you. Many times we think we have failed in a situation when spiritually we have succeeded. For example, perhaps your answer reflects the year your marriage failed. You may believe this to be a failure. You may view that time in your life as a black mark on your report card. However, if you look beneath the surface of your life at that point, you may see that you actually grew in your spiritual development. Since we are here to learn and advance our spiritual growth, perhaps you need to see the success in this situation, for indeed you grew. Experiencing a traumatic situation and then being able to let it go when it is complete is a big success. The only failure is when you fail to grow. This is a simple, yet profound, question.

(2) What spiritual goal do I need to accomplish this year?

Our spiritual growth is important. And growth is achieved most effectively when we have clear goals to direct us. You may wish to seek guidance as to what personal spiritual goal would be appropriate for you at this time. This is the type of question that might lend itself to follow-up questions for clarification as well. For example, if your higher self indicates you need to learn to give love, you may wish to follow up with questions that will clarify the specific areas of your life or people in your life in need of love from you. Anytime you feel you do not have enough information from your higher self, do not hesitate to ask additional questions. But remember that your follow up questions need to be very direct in order to receive this clarification. The more you ask, the more you receive.

(3) What am I pulling in my wagon?

We inhibit personal progress in life by dragging behind us year after year old baggage that we should have left behind long ago. If we could empty our wagons of these weighty memories, problems, missed opportunities and other regrets, we would be able to move ahead in future days free to explore and experience what life has in store. In order to free ourselves from these burdens, we first must identify them. Often we have no idea what anchors we insist upon dragging along with us.

Find out what things from your past you are still clinging to by asking your higher self, "What am I pulling in my wagon?" You may be surprised at the answer. It could be helpful in focusing on a situation in which you are having problems but cannot understand why. For example, if you see a person from your past— perhaps an ex-spouse or a business partner— you have not finished dealing with your emotions regarding that relationship or situation. I have had successful businessmen as clients who learned from this exercise that they were still trying to please a demanding father, who had died many years before.

If you find that you are pulling a watch in your wagon, you are overly concerned about time. You might have grown up with an overemphasis on punctuality. Certainly this is a virtue, but there are people today who waste two hours before any appointment worrying about being on time. More important for most of us, an obsession with time can affect the spontaneity of life. A ring in your wagon means that you want to blend, bond or complete a circle that you feel is unfinished in your life.

If we can identify the objects weighting us down, we promote proper growth in two ways. First, we weaken the hold that this obstacle may have on us just by removing its mystery. When a problem is exposed to sunlight, the dissolving process begins. Second, by knowing our adversary we can devise a means of challenging and defeating him. It is helpful to learn exactly what you are pulling in your wagon.

(4) What do I do in my life that causes unnecessary turmoil?

Can you see the forest for the trees? Maybe not. Often we let procrastination, over-aggressiveness, suspicion or some other personality trait create severe turmoil in our lives. Yet through either habit or denial we fail to recognize what is causing life to be so unstable. Your higher self can give you the answer that your conscious mind has concealed from you.

Simply ask your higher self what you are doing that creates unnecessary turmoil in your life. Ask it to be as direct as possible. If you see a calculator, you're always keeping a running tab. You have trouble letting things go. If you see yourself stomping your foot, turning red in the face or knotting up your fist, you are harboring some anger about something. This anger is creating unnecessary turmoil for you.

This question can strip away the camouflage and reveal to you how you may open your life to its full potential.

(5) What is my state of mind at this time in my life?

Are you open to new ideas and opportunities? Is your engine in overdrive? Or are you temporarily operating in low gear? What is your present attitude toward life? You can even ask this question on a daily basis to determine the type of day to expect. In determining your state of mind regularly, you may choose to postpone certain plans until your state of mind is more conducive to fulfilling those plans successfully. For example, if you wish to confront and coach an employee about certain weak areas in his performance and your state of mind symbol is a refrigerator, you may wish to postpone that discussion. A refrigerator would probably indicate that you are in a cold, rigid frame of mind—not the best attitude for offering constructive criticism to an employee. The following day you might see an open book, indicating an openness in your life, one of learning not to hide inner feelings. On that day you may be better equipped to motivate an employee.

This question is an effective aid in understanding ourselves. Quite often plans cannot and should not be changed regardless of the answer. Even so, the symbol provides a better understanding of our mental climate at a particular moment and gives us a basis for guarding against unproductive responses and attitudes. I do not at all suggest that anyone become a slave to the fluctuations of his state of mind. This exercise is not a crutch but a means of achieving a keener understanding of ourselves. An attorney friend of mine had a client who wanted to manipulate her court date so that it coincided with her most favorable astrological reading. Needless to say, the judicial system was not going to incorporate the litigants' astrological forecasts into its calendaring system.

This question provides understanding and guidance. Sometimes a slight change of plans is feasible. At other times it is helpful merely to be wary of certain states of mind as we proceed as planned. Either way an objective revelation of your current state of mind is useful.

(6) How does my cage look?

Your cage is a symbol of your life, so pay attention to the details of this image. Is the cage neat or messy? Does it have many decorations? Is it simple or full of valuables? A neat, orderly cage signifies a neat, orderly life. You are taking care of things as they need to be handled. A cluttered cage indicates that your life is cluttered as well. You are dealing with a lot of issues. You need to get rid of some things in your world. I find that people's visual cages range from the very ornate, complete with chandeliers and candelabras, to the very stark and simple. The former symbolizes one who relishes attention, drama and the finer things in life. If a person's cage contains lots of valuable objects, this person is aware of what things in life are important to him. A simple cage, on the other hand, logically reflects a person with a simple and direct attitude toward life. This person is in control, and little disturbs his world. A white floor in the cage symbolizes a spiritual base.

If you have envisioned a bed in your cage, this means that you are in need of rest. A swing suggests that you may go back and forth too much. You have difficulty making decisions. A ball somewhere in the cage means you are flexible, just as rubber is flexible. Some have seen a candle in their cages. The candle itself represents your physical self while the glow of the candle is your spiritual being. The glow is light and warmth. It serves as protection for you. If you are ever afraid, light a candle. Similarly, if the floor has straw or feathers on it, this means you have support.

Suppose you have seen yourself inside your cage with the door closed. As you might expect, this tells you that you are feeling confined. Although you may not even have admitted it to your conscious self, there is some part of your life that is causing you to feel boxed in at the moment. This may involve money, your career or a relationship. Sometimes we have so much time and energy invested in a part of life that we cling to it like a lifeboat. It takes our subconscious to tap us on the shoulder and tell us to find a way out.

What does your symbolic cage say about your life?

(7) What is a good energy source for me?

Your answer to this question should be simple to interpret. Whatever you receive as your symbol is exactly what you need to supply you with greater resources of energy. Some common energy sources include sun, food, water, clay, art, sleep, a crystal, the moon, and fire. One client of mine received sand as her response to this question. She lived by the beach but never took the time to go there. Now, whenever she is low on energy, she drives to the beach and has direct contact with the sand either through walking barefoot or just sitting and experiencing the sand around her. She returns from these experiences completely re-energized.

(8) What is my greatest learning at this time in my life?

The answer to this question should come in a single symbol which is self-explanatory. For example, if you are in the midst of a painful situation and you receive a cactus as your symbol, you are reminded to look past the pain of the "thorns" in order to find the nourishment or growth of this painful situation. Always keep in mind what the symbol means to you. Books suggest more learning through reading. Toys tell you to play more. The sun indicates healing and warmth. Suitcases reveal travel.

Additional Questions for Your Higher Self

Use the following questions, or questions of your own, to continue and expand your dialogue with your higher self.

What kind of year am I having?

What techniques will best help me focus on the important things in my life?

What is the best scene for me to visualize in my meditations?

I see an empty picture frame. What do I need to put into it?

What from my past is holding me back?

What is a good, calming relaxation symbol for me?

How can I best understand myself?

What can I expect from my relationship with _____ ?

What was my lesson with _____ ?

Give me a prediction for next month.

What is my greatest fear? How can I overcome it?

When things are hectic, how can I calm myself?

What foods do I need to eliminate from my diet?

What is a problem that I create for myself?

What nursery rhyme best describes me?

What is my greatest source of strength in the physical world?

Who is or was my greatest teacher?

What can I do to add greater balance to my life?

How can I bring more fun into my life?

What emotion do I have trouble releasing?

How does my higher self see me at this time?

What symbol represents me spiritually? physically? emotionally? intellectually?

CHAPTER 21

Aligning with the Flow

The symbol is neither abstract nor concrete, neither rational
nor irrational, neither real nor unreal. It is always both.

Carl G. Jung

Your higher self can give you direction through various media. There is a direction for you to walk today that will give you more satisfaction and productivity than any other. We all have the freedom to choose any path we wish, and with dedication we can make it work. But life is easier when we are aligned with the millions of other energy forces that are at work in this world of ours. As I have previously suggested, the difference lies in paddling with the current versus paddling upstream against the flow of life's river.

I have found the following exercises to be helpful in making life's choices, both large and small. They have been refined and utilized through the years as a means of expression of the higher self.

Numbered Guidance

We don't need a telegraph station to receive messages from another dimension. Your higher self can direct you through the use of a pair of dice. The numbers that you roll with these dice can give you useful clues to upcoming events during the day. Roll them in the morning to see what to expect from your day. The number you roll is not left to chance, for your higher self is guiding the outcome of your roll. There are no accidents. If you know the energy surrounding your day, you can then work with it instead of against it.

INTERPRETATION: Here are the meanings to all of the possible combinations that you might roll. They will give you some understanding of what to expect from this day.

2   STAY CLOSE. Today is not a time to reach out. This is not a day for new beginnings. Allow the Universe to give you what you need. Do not become impatient with routine. You may feel like an observer.

3   DISTURBANCE IN RELATIONSHIPS. This day will bring relationships that still need work. You may repeat learning in dealing with others. You need to focus on others, not yourself. It is a day of "giving of yourself."

4   WISDOM, CHANGE, OPPORTUNITY, FINANCIAL GAIN. You are the leader and will come out on top. This is a good day for investing of yourself, money or time.

5   NEW INSIGHT, GETTING RID OF THE OLD. Today is a day of learning. People will enter your life as teachers. Listen to your day. You will be forced to let go of old patterns, people or things. Look within for new attitudes.

6 BALANCE. Work with a schedule. Keep an open mind. Do not overwork issues. Have fun, relax, create and find a quiet time to connect to your God. These four things will give you balance.

7 STAND TALL. Do not let others overwhelm you. Take a stand on what you believe. Be proud, direct and assertive. You will see magic performed today.

8 CARE FOR THE PAST. Shadows from your past reappear today. You may run into old acquaintances, old situations that need attention, or you may need to repeat something. Reflect on the past.

9 YOU ARE THE HEALER. You will see how wonderful and wise you are. Reach out to those in need. Touch the souls of all you cross, and you will indeed be blessed.

10 OPEN TO FEELINGS WITHIN YOU, MENTAL WORK. This is a day of self-discovery. Pay attention to yourself. You will experience extreme highs and lows. Concentration is strong. This is a day to learn.

11 ONE HURDLE AFTER ANOTHER. This is not a day to test your patience. Take one step at a time. Persevere. Keep your sense of humor, and you will find the day to be productive.

12 NEED COMPANIONSHIP. Friends and family will be important. Truly value those in your life. Do not be alone this day.

It's All in the Cards

Your higher self can also direct you through the use of ordinary playing cards. Select from a deck of playing cards seven cards numbered one through seven. The particular suit does not matter. Shuffle the cards a few times as you ask your higher self a question. Silently repeat the question over and over again as you shuffle. When you are ready, turn over the top card and determine your answer based on the interpretations outlined below.

Card: *Meaning:*

1   Go forward. This also can be used as a "yes" answer.

2   Hesitate. The timing is wrong.

3   More knowledge will be gained from the pursuit than from the outcome itself. If you look at the experience as a whole, it will bring depth of character and spirit. The lesson is learned by experiencing the moment.

4   This is not a path you must walk and never will be. The story has yet to be told.

5   This is a lesson in persistence. Patience is required. How badly do you want it?

6   Shake it loose. It has absorbed you. You are no longer objective.

7   This will melt away in time. It is not long lasting.

Remember, the meanings given here are general indications. Trust your intuition and ask for additional symbols to be shown you to clarify specific issues if you like, using the techniques and principles you have already learned in this book.

CHAPTER 22

An Expanding of Science

*In the entire history of science, it is hard to find a discovery
of comparable consequence to the discovery of the power
of unconscious beliefts as a gateway—or an obstacle
to the hidden mind, and its untapped potentialities.
With considerable justification,we could speak of
the widespread adoption of this discovery by science and
society as a "second Copernican revolution."*
Willis Harman, Ph.D.; Howard Rheingold

*The major task of the twentieth century will be to explore
the unconscious, to investigate the subsoil of the mind.*
Henry Bergson

Accepting the messages of internal and external symbols becomes more and more important as our physical world becomes more complex. It provides some focus in a society that pulls at us from every direction. Yet some are hesitant to untie their moorings to the past and allow this compass to lead them. They suggest that it has not achieved status as a scientific principle.

Symbology is an effective method of expanding our awareness by utilizing a potential for communication that has existed from the beginning of time. It is a proven technique that is consistent with all laws of nature. In fact, an awareness of the interrelationships in the universe provides an important piece to life's puzzle. Contrary to any concern that this approach departs from what we have come to call "scientific thought," it helps us to understand our world more completely.

The question arises simply because in recent decades we have tended to reduce our concept of "science" into knowledge that can be quantified by the use of test tubes, microscopes and other means of measurement. Originally the term science had referred to the accumulation of all human knowledge. It embraced an openness to new ideas and an expansion of concepts. As the twentieth century has seen an explosion of scientific breakthroughs beyond what mankind has ever experienced before, there has been both a celebration of science and an undercurrent of uncertainty as to whether we as individuals can keep pace with the world. As we have reinvented our physical world each decade of this century, there has been a notable tendency to put a fence around what we call science.

The fear of reaching beyond the known and tangible was illustrated by columnist Wiley Hilburn in a story about a father who had been trying to get his small son to sleep for several hours. It had been a long day, and the father looked forward to unwinding quietly, perhaps watching a little television and finishing a novel. He finally got the child into bed upstairs. A few minutes later he heard a familiar small voice from the top of the stairs. His little son begged him to come up and lie down with him until he could get to sleep.

"I'm scared . . . please come up here with me." The father desperately wanted an hour to himself. "Don't be afraid," he called back to his son. "God will take care of you."

Silence from the top of the stairs. The father breathed a sigh of relief and turned on the television.

Then, from that same top of the stairs, a tiny, shadowy figure spoke. "I'd rather have somebody with skin."

The father smiled, turned off the TV and walked up the stairs.

Uncertainty about the unknown afflicts adults as well. One way of protecting our security in a rapidly changing world is to confine our definition of science. We have come to admit into the scientific arena only that which can be tested and measured with precision.

This is unnecessarily restrictive and out of step with the traditional concept of science. Daniel J. Boorstin in *The Exploring Spirit* tells us that, "Dazzled by the sudden and spectacular growth of knowledge through science, we are tempted to forget that the rise of science was also a new recognition of the extent of the unknown." Boorstin relates that Sir Isaac Newton, a pioneer in the early scientific movement, wrote near the end of his life:

> I do not know what I may appear to the world, but to myself I seem to have been only like a boy playing on the seashore, and diverting myself now and then finding a smoother pebble or a prettier shell than ordinary, whilst the great ocean of truth lay all undiscovered before me.

An expansive concept of science allows for the existence of this ocean of truth as yet undiscovered as well as the pebbles and shells that we do see and comprehend.

Admittedly, there is a certain security that could be derived from boxing in our world. We can construct walls of the existing empirical knowledge and live out our days in the thought that all that is known is all there is to know.

But have we come to this planet only to exist and feel secure? Those of us who believe that life achieves its purpose only in learning and experiencing and stretching to its limits find that opening up to the voice of the inner self is an exploration consistent with the searches of Copernicus and Galileo and is entirely consistent with a proper concept of scientific exploration.

If we take in the whole of the scientific movement, we must not discount the exploration of the unconscious simply because it defies measurement in a modern test tube. It also produces its own proof of validity. One client was listening to a tape recording of one of my Learning to See workshops while he was idly looking through books in his personal library at home. Repeatedly as he took a book off the shelf and turned randomly to a page, the first word he saw on that page was also being discussed on the tape. For example, he tells me that I was talking about the meaning of the symbol "8" on the clock in the "What Time Is on Your Clock?" exercise in this book when he opened a book to a chapter discussing an author's eighth point in a series. As he opened other books there was a correspondence between the spoken and written words as well.

This surely suggests a part of the ocean of truth that Newton understood was yet to be explored. Inclusion in a science book is not the sine qua non of reality. We have been able to measure our solar system and its cyclical movement enough to send objects into space and bring them back. We have learned enough about the tiny atom to destroy portions of our civilization. We must not close our minds to the potential of the higher self merely because it does not seem to be measurable by any of our conventional yardsticks. Its presence is here nevertheless. Its profile can be seen in the lives of people as they anticipate events and as they are directed into the deep current of life and away from the rocky shoals. It casts its shadow in daily events that we often mark up as coincidences. It makes itself known in the quality of life that is available to all of us.

CHAPTER 23

Looking Ahead

Are you up to your destiny?

Hamlet

Hopefully the preceding exercises have opened doors of new awareness for you. Practice will enable you to perfect your ability to learn from your higher self. Knowledge leads to growth. We are in this life together to experience and grow.

Take your time in getting to know your higher self. Time is only an illusion anyway. We have eternity before us. Even in terms of time as we know it, there is no hurry. In the exercises I have described in this book, certain time periods are suggested. These are merely for your convenience. If they are helpful, use them. If not, don't let them restrict you.

You will find yourself stretching long unused mental muscles. You will be exploring new ways of viewing your world. Let these concepts seep into your consciousness at their own pace. For some this will be a natural and speedy transition, soon leading to lengthy periods of new awareness. For others there may be only brief glimpses of the broader universe before daily reality intrudes again. Either way you are moving forward.

You may wish to make immediate use of the various exercises as part of a consistent daily program. Or the rhythm of your world at this moment may incline you to select a different pace for practice. Whatever is right for you is the best way to apply these principles in your life. Each of us is an intricate assemblage of experiences, desires, ambitions and thought patterns as well as a physical presence. As these facets of our being shift or expand, our individual readiness to talk with the higher self moves to the forefront.

Life is meant to be simple. If it is hard, we are doing something wrong. If doors are closing, we are in the wrong corridor. Your inner self can direct you. Listen to what it tells you. When you find the rhythm of life, everything is right. You awaken every morning with excitement and enthusiasm for the day. There is a life-style, an occupation, an environment that ideally suits your temperament, your talents and your needs. Your inner self will help you find it.

Beyond this, your inner guidance will reveal to you the attitude with which to live your life. There is no reason to let the world control you. This is your world. It was made for you. Use all its dimensions, and make it yours.

I hope the exercises in this book will become your own magic carpet to the worlds of awareness that await you. Each time you open the door to your higher self, you take another step toward your destiny.

When we uncross our arms and allow the higher self to guide us, we open the skylight of our creativity, our joy and a zest for life in all its dimensions.

Your Personal Symbol Dictionary

In working with symbols, the hardest thing to do is to trust your first thought or feeling. We always want to analyze everything before we allow it to flow from our conscious minds. In becoming your own interpreter, you must overcome that impulse to analyze, and trust your first response. Record it without any thought as to whether or not it makes sense. Then after receiving all the symbols being presented, go back and analyze their meaning to you.

The symbols offered in this book is a listing of some of the most common symbols I have encountered in my work as an interpreter. This is not to say that these are the authoritative symbols and their corresponding interpretations. Quite the contrary. They are listed here as an example and as an aid to you. Feel comfortable in referring to my list at the outset of developing your inner communication skills. However, always rely on your own instinctual interpretations over the ones listed here. Since you will be receiving your symbols from your higher self, it is important to use your own interpretations.

Over the last few years I have kept a running tab of symbols for my work. Even now I am surprised with a new one from time to time. I simply interpret what it means to me and add it to my dictionary. I encourage you to do the same.

Common Symbols

Symbol/Image:	Interpretation:
AIRPLANE	trip by air
ALCOHOL BOTTLE	drinking problem or addiction to chemicals
ALLIGATOR	eaten alive
ALTAR	a need for reverence
AMUSEMENT PARK	fun in life
ANCHOR	stability, holding still
ANGEL	guardian protection shown
ANKLE	area that is weak
ANT	busy, busy, busy; persistent
ANTENNA	reaching beyond, picking up easily from another
APPLAUSE	pleasure or approval shown
APPLE	food for thought
APRON STRINGS	won't let go or grow up
ARCH	a need to bend
ARROW	focus, aim
ARM	extension for support
ASHES	dissolve
ATHLETE	athletic ability or a discipline
ATTIC	being mental
ATTIC (cluttered)	need to clear out thinking
AUDIENCE	will be in front of people in some capacity

AUTUMN	used to reference time
AX	sharpness; cut to the quick
BABY	a birth or a new beginning
BACK	back problem; burdens being carried as if there is a load on the back
BACKWARD WORDS	learning disability
BAGGAGE	travel
BALCONY	rising above; overseeing
BALD	used in describing a person
BALL	balance
BALL, BOUNCING	a need to be flexible
BALLOON	light or lifted up
BANK	money
BASEMENT	hidden; not yet shown; the subconscious
BATH	cleansing
BATTERY	energy needed or offered
BATTLE	conflict
BEACH	needs to relax or have fun; peace
BEARD	cover up or a description of a person
BEAVER	gnaws on things too long
BED	a need for rest
BEE	will sting or already stung
BELL	needs to be heard
BELT	feeling squeezed in a situation or relationship
BIBLE	religious person or attitude
BICYCLE	exercise, balance
BINOCULARS	clearer focus
BIRD	freedom; messenger; guardian spirit
BIRTH	new beginning
BLANKET	protection
BLIND	cannot see things clearly or wishes not to see
BLINDFOLDED	not seeing something

BLIZZARD	out of control
BLOOD	life force being given or taken away
BOAT	movement
BODY PART	possible health issue with body part shown
BONE	enticement or health description
BOOK	knowledge or new learning
BOTTLE	a need to nurture
BOW (ribbon)	to reward, gift, decoration
BOW	humble
BOX	confinement
BOXES (packed)	change in home
BRAID	twisted or tangled up
BRAIN	refers to the intellect
BRAKE	slow down
BRANCH	extension
BREAD	nourishment; or to avoid wheat in diet
BRICK	hard as a rock; a blow
BRIDE	new beginning; a blending
BRIDGE	cross over or a connection made
BROKEN HEART	hurt feelings
BROOK	serene
BROOM	sweep up
BUBBLE	soft protection
BUD	opening; just starting
BUDDHA	the need to be still or to meditate
BUG	little things get to you; nuisance
BULB (lighted)	shines like a star
BULL	headstrong
BULL IN CHINA SHOP	moves too quickly through life; not cautious
BULLDOZER	goes at things head first
BURP	digestive problems or rejects

BUS	movement
BUTCHER	chops things to death
BUTTER	spread out; blend; smooth
BUTTERFLY	freedom
CACTUS	painful lesson; you must get through the sticky part to find the nourishment
CAGE	confinement
CAKE	celebration; "have your cake and eat it too"
CALENDAR	used as a time reference
CAMEL	great endurance
CANDLE	burning the candle at both ends
CANDY	treat; sweet
CANE	crutch; given assistance, support
CAP	limiting thoughts
CAR	refers to the physical body
CARDS	new game in life; lighten up; "he's a card"
CARPENTER	creative, can build something from nothing
CARROT	enticement
CASKET	death in some part of life
CAT	a female energy; mystical or always land on your feet
CAVE	to go within; something hidden
CEILING	keep a lid on your thinking
CEMETERY	ending
CHAIN	connection made; chain of events; held back, "in chains"
CHAIR	support
CHAMPAGNE	celebration
CHEWING	contemplating a situation
CHICKEN	raised on a farm, wants country life or cowardly

CHILDREN	needs to be more childlike or is a child
CHOIR	sing praise
CHOKING	difficulty swallowing something
CIGAR/CIGARETTE	descriptive of smoker, allergic
CIRCLE	completion, balance, connect
CIRCUS	confusion
CLAMP	closed up
CLAY	leaves a stain, may stay for awhile
CLIFF	pushed to a limit, standing on the edge; a gamble
CLIMB	progress
CLOSET	hidden, withdrawn, not yet seen
CLOTHESLINE	air out
CLOUD	confusion
CLOWN	many faces, wears a mask
COAT	protection
COBWEBS	caught up in old patterns
COFFEE	refers to caffeine
COFFIN	dead
COINS	money
COLORS	
BLACK	morbid, depressing
BLUE	calmness, wholeness; spiritual insight; vision
BROWN	physical, earthy
GOLD	spiritual clarity
GREEN	healing, balance
PINK	love, desire
PURPLE	regal, royalty, power
RED	anger, high energy, dramatic, aggressive
SILVER	old wisdom
WHITE	spiritual; purity
YELLOW	mental

COMPASS	focus on where you are going
CONCRETE HEART	hard-hearted
CONDUCTOR	leader
COOK	creative; talent for cooking
CORK	to plug, to block
CORNER	feels backed in
COUCH	a need to relax
COW	put out to pasture
CRACK	broken
CRADLE	needs to be rocked; goes back and forth
CREAM	good; will rise to the top; sweet
CROSS	burden; religious; crossroads
CRUTCH	support
CRYSTAL BALL	intuition, insight
CUT	wounded
DAM	overwhelmed
DANCE	movement
DARK	hidden
DART	aim and focus; dodging something
DECK	outside of a situation
DEER	innocence
DEVIL	mean, negative
DESK	study; detail work
DIAMOND	will shine, sparkle; indestructible
DIARY	a need to record
DICE	take a chance
DIPLOMA	finishing
DISH (empty)	no nourishment
DISH (full)	nourishment
DITCH	wallowing
DOCTOR	healing; also could mean a checkup is needed
DOG	playful, childlike; a guide

DOLL	emotionally fragile or immature
DOOR (opened)	a passage; opportunity
DOOR (closed)	blocked
DONKEY	stubborn
DOVE	spiritual freedom; peace
DRAGON	anger
DRAWER	opening new parts of self
DRIVEWAY	path
DROWNING	drowning in emotions
DRUM	need to be heard
DUCK	let things roll off back; don't react; waddle
DWARF	feels small, ego low
EAGLE	soar
EAR	need to listen
EGG	fertility; hatching something new, but patience needed
ELASTIC BAND	stretched in some capacity
ELBOW	bend
ELEPHANT	larger than life
ELEVATOR	raising your consciousness
ENVELOPE	concealed, hidden
EYE	"I"; your Higher Self
EYES SQUINTING	trying to get a better look or a need to see more clearly
FAN	a breath of fresh air
FARM	country
FAUCET (on)	flowing; yes
FAUCET (off)	blocked; no
FEATHER	gift from your guidance coming soon
FENCE	barrier
FIGHT	confrontation, defensive
FILM	repeated pattern progressing
FINGER	direction given

FINGERS (being pried open)	difficulty letting go
FINGER (pointing)	criticism
FIRE	energy or destruction
FISH	Christianity
FISHING ROD	fish for new things in life
FIST	on the defensive
FLAG (waving)	make peace
FLAME	energy offered
FLOOD	overwhelmed
FLOWER	unfoldment, opening up; will grow
FLUTE	softness; needs to be quietly heard
FOG	confusion
FOOT	foundation
FOREHEAD (wrinkled)	worries too much
FOX	slyness
FROG	sit and leap, sit and leap; has difficulty going with the flow
FUR	protection; warm and snug
GARBAGE	trash in life or situation
GARDEN	pleasant, peaceful situation
GATE	an opening or a passing through
GLASS	can see through a situation; crystal clear
GLASSES	needs help seeing something more clearly
GLOVE	protection
GLUE	stuck
GOAT	not accepting responsibility
GOLD COINS	extra money
GRADUATION GOWN	a completion
GRAPES	bunching
GROCERY STORE	choices offered

GUITAR	musical ability
HAMMER	beats things to death
HAMMOCK	a need to be lazy
HAND (palm up)	needs to receive
HAND (palm down)	needs to give
HANDS OVER MOUTH	be quiet
HANDS AROUND MOUTH	speak out
HANDS HOLDING SOMEONE UP (under the arms)	support
HANDCUFF	restricted
HANDLE	help offered; something to hold on to
HANDS OVER EARS	not hearing, not wanting to hear
HARP	sweet, harmony, celestial
HAT	control your thinking
HEART	love
HEN	mothering
HILL	climbing; hurdle to cross
HOE	dig in; turn things over; get to the bottom of it
HORN	make noise, make someone pay attention
HORSE	strength
HOSPITAL	healing
HOUSE (cluttered)	scattered thoughts; self, state of consciousness
HURDLE	a challenge to overcome
INDIAN	a guide or teacher
INK	will leave a stain; permanent
IRON	needs to get the wrinkles out of a situation, to smooth out
JAIL	confinement
JAR	on the inside looking out; too close to the situation

JESUS	spiritual guide, religious person
JOURNAL	needs to keep a log; record needed
JUDGE	too judgmental
JUGGLE	trying to do too much
JUMP	get over something
JUNGLE	confusion
KANGAROO	jumps from one thing to another
KEY	unlocking the inner self
KING	feels superior
KISS	affection shown
KITCHEN	needs to prepare; whip up new things
KITE	freedom, flying high
KNEEL	humble
KNIFE	sharp edge; cutting a new direction
KNITTING	to put together; to blend
KNOCKING	a new opportunity
KNOTS	frustration
LABORATORY	a testing time or situation
LADDER	raising consciousness; changing thoughts
LAMB	humble; warmth, gentleness; sacrifice
LAMP (with shade)	does not let others see his/her light
LAMP (no shade)	lets everyone see his/her light; exposed
LANDSLIDE	losing your footing or foundation; rug is being pulled out from underneath
LAUNDRY	need to cleanse; always looks at the dirty side of life
LAXATIVE	a need to release
LEAVES (on tree)	growth
LEAVES (falling off tree)	need to detach
LEATHER	durable, tough
LEG	foundation, strength to stand

LEMON	bitter, sour
LETTER	information coming
LIBRARY	new learning
LICENSE	permission given
LIGHTNING	sharp awareness, bolt of energy; pay attention
LIMB	new path or direction; "out on a limb"
LION	courage
LIQUID	dissolved
LOCK	secure
LUGGAGE (packing)	travel opportunity
LUMBER	a need to create something new
MACHINE	mechanically inclined
MAGICIAN	has magical ability, can create
MAGNET	intense drawing toward; magnetism
MAKEUP	covering up
MANURE	a pile of nothing
MAP	direction
MASK	many different faces; moody
MEDICINE	medication needed
MERRY-GO-ROUND	going in circles, not moving forward, no accomplishments
MESSY DESK	scattered
MICROSCOPE	blow things out of proportion
MILK	allergic to dairy products
MINUS SIGN	negative or a no answer
MIRROR	need to see self
MONEY	values or extra money
MONSTER	making something out to be worse than it is; repressed feelings
MOON	magic; romance
MOUNTAIN	challenge to overcome
MOUSE	quiet; reserved and still

MOVIE	need to sit back and take another view of you or your life
MOVING VAN	change in home
MUD	stuck in a rut
MULE	stubborn
MUMMY	not for real
MUSCLE	strength shown
MUSEUM	on exhibit
MUSICAL NOTE	musical or harmonious
NAIL	tough as nails or the need to focus
NEEDLE	sticky, painful, difficult situation; get the point
NEST	comfortable home, snug surroundings
NET	caught up in
NOSE	nosy or being led around
NUDE	feels exposed
NUMBER ONE	leader
NUN	sees things as black or white, yes or no; spiritual teacher
NURSE	healer
NUTS	shell, protected; "crazy"
OCTOPUS	reaching in all directions; somewhat scattered
OIL	slippery
ONION	many layers of self or situation, or needs to cry
OPERATION	need to delve into something
ORCHARD	fruitful situation
ORCHESTRA	need to hear; listen to the sweetness
ORNAMENT	added benefit or gift
OWL	sees all
PACKAGE	gift or a surprise
PADDLE	moving forward
PAINT	new coat of life offered; face lift

PAPER	tears easily; extremely sensitive
PARACHUTE	support from spiritual kingdom
PARADE	on display
PARROT	repeats patterns or lessons
PARTY	celebration
PASSENGER	not in control of a situation
PATH	direction to follow
PATIO	on the outside looking in
PATTERN	new direction
PATTING SELF ON BACK	self-praise
PEARL	wisdom
PEDESTAL	lifting above
PEN	writing ability; permanency
PENGUIN	black or white, yes or no
PENDULUM	back and forth; no decision made
PENIS	sexual
PEPPER	add seasoning to your life or situation
PERFUME	sweetness
PIANO	musical ability or entertainment
PIE	a piece of the pie; something good
PIER	extension or overlooking something
PIG	wallow in a situation
PIGEON	messenger
PILLAR	strength
PILLOW, FLUFFED	things are made easier
PILOT	in control
PIN CUSHION	painful situation
PIRATE	rebel
PLASTIC	artificial, flexible
PLOW	turning things over; dig in
PLUMBER	the need to look at the emotions
POCKET	hiding something
POISON	not a positive influence

POLICE	cautious or assistance offered
POND	emotions contained
POPCORN	jumps from one thing to another
POPE	spiritual leader
PORCH	on the outside looking in
POSTER	exposure; promote self or situation
POSTMAN	message offer
POWDER	blessing
PRAYING HANDS	serenity, a need to pray
PREGNANT WOMAN	something new about to happen
PRESIDENT	leader
PRIEST	religious person
PRINCE	a genuine person
PRINCESS	wants to be treated special; sensitive
PRISON	confinement
PURSE	housing your values
PURSE (with money)	extra money
PURSE (empty)	be cautious with spending
PUPPET	being controlled
PUZZLE	delicate situation; everything had to fit
PYRAMID	power or energy offered
QUEEN	wants to be treated well, feels superior
QUILT	covering, protection
RABBIT	has no patience; quick movement; will not last
RABBIT IN HAT	magical powers
RACCOON	tunnel vision
RADAR	alert; be aware
RADIO	communication
RAGS	subject has no value or is worn
RAILROAD TRACKS	direction given or should be followed
RAIN	cleansing

RAINBOW	clarity, beauty; nature's way of saying "thank you"
RAM	take the bull by the horns
RAT	not someone to trust
RAZOR	sharp; will cut you if not cautious
RECORD	things being repeated
REFRIGERATOR	cold in emotions
RIPPLE IN WATER	hurt feelings
RING	bond, unite, blend
RIVER	flows indefinitely
ROAD	path, direction
ROBOT	stiff, artificial
ROCK	solid
ROCKET	taking off; new adventure
ROOF	thinking must be or is controlled
ROOSTER	boastful; "head of the henhouse"
ROOT	depth; getting to the core
ROPE	held back or confined; "end of my rope"
ROSARY	pray; draw on power of prayer
ROSE	unfold; opening up
RUBBER	flexibility
RULER	straight as an arrow; discipline
RUG	foundation
RUST	old behavior, old habits
SAD FACE	disappointment
SADDLE	comfortable
SAILBOAT	movement, relaxation
SAND	change
SAW	situation or person goes back and forth
SCALES	balance
SCAR	hurt feelings
SCARECROW	guarded, fearful

SCHOOL	structured learning
SCIENTIST	investigative
SCORPION	poison
SEAL (with ball on nose)	a need to balance
SEAM	a need to blend and come together
SEED	starting a new beginning
SEESAW	highs and lows
SHADE	unable to see total picture
SHADOW	past
SHAMPOO	clean up thinking
SHAVE	remove mask
SHARK	eaten alive
SHEEP	cowardly
SHELL	a cocoon; very protected
SHIELD	defense
SHOE	foundation
SHOULDER	a chip on the shoulder
SHOWER	cleansing
SILK	smooth as silk
SINGING	joyful
SKATE	glides easily
SKELETON	part of your past
SKIN	probable skin condition
SKY (clear)	smooth sailing
SKY (cloudy)	confusion
SMOKE	confusion
SNAIL	slow
SNAKE	sneaky; might bite
SNEEZE	rejection
SNOW	cold reaction
SOAP	cleansing
SOLDIER	rigid

SPINE	probable health issue with spine or stiffen up; be strong
SPONGE	absorbs easily
SPOON	spoon fed; things are easy
SQUARE	boxed in, confined
SQUIRREL	nuisance; always looking and searching
STAGE	wants to be on stage; always out front
STAIRS	raising consciousness
STAR	shines like a star; success
STATUE	stiff
STEEL	sturdy
STEERING WHEEL	must take control
STORM	tremendous activity
STUMP	block
SUBMARINE	down under; not yet come to life
SUITCASE	travel opportunity
SUN	energy given or warmth offered
SWAMP	messy situation or relationship
SWAN	graceful
SWORD	protection; shield
SYRINGE	sucks life from you
SYRUP	overly sweet; not to be trusted
TAIL	the end
TABLE	something offered
TANGLE	knotted situation; confused feelings
TAPESTRY	very complex
TAPPING FOOT	impatient
TARGET	a need to focus
TEARS	sadness; cleansing
TEDDY BEAR	a real softy
TEETH	need to bite into something; possible health issue with teeth
TELEPHONE	communication

TELEVISION	exposure
TEMPLE	sacred
TENT	protection
THORN	difficulty
THREAD	a very fine path
THROAT	expression
TIDAL WAVE	feeling of being overwhelmed
TIGHTROPE	path is narrow and difficult
TIGER	a handful
TIRES (flat)	out of energy
TOILET	elimination
TONGUE (moving)	talks a lot
TONGUE (holding)	must hold your tongue
TOWER	strength
TOY	a need to play more
TRAIN	follow the leader or movement
TRAP	caught
TREADMILL	never gets anything accomplished; goes round and round
TREE	growth
TRIANGLE	energy
TUG OF WAR	caught in the middle; will not let go; refusing to compromise; moving back and forth
TURTLE	slow-moving
TWO BRAINS	can think of more than one thing at a time
UMBRELLA	spiritual protection; held up
V	victory
VACUUM CLEANER	feeling sucked up
VAULT	locked up inside; unable to release emotions
VEHICLE (stuck)	stuck in a rut
VINE	cling or hold on
VOLCANO	explosion

VOMIT	rejection
WAGON (full)	carrying a heavy load of responsibility
WAGON (empty)	may feel unfulfilled
WALL	blocked
WALLET	usually concerns money; money coming is full wallet, money tight is empty wallet
WAND	the ability to create, magical ability
WAR	conflict
WASHING HANDS	should not be a part of situation or relationship
WATCH	too concerned with time
WATER	always relates to the emotions
WATERFALL	may become overwhelmed
WAVE	ride the highs and lows
WAX	slick
WEAPON	tool to protect
WEAVE	ins and outs
WEB	caught up in something
WELL	depth of self
WHALE	larger than life
WHEAT	nourishment
WHEEL	a need to control
WHIP	abusive; hard as nails, tough; beats a horse to death; driving force
WIND	movement
WINDOW	can see through something; a pathway from the physical world to the spiritual world; your spirit
WINGS	taking off; reborn
WHITE-ROBED PERSON	spiritual
WIRE	connect
WOLF	the need to howl

WOOL	warm and snug
WOOD	solid
WRECK	disruption
YAWN	bored
YARN	goes on forever
YO-YO	highs and lows
ZEBRA	sees things as black or white, yes or no
ZIPPER	shut up
ZOO	lacking order

References

1. Bloodworth, Dennis, *The Chinese Looking Glass*, Farrar, Straus and Giroux (1967), pp. 210-213.

2. Boorstin, Daniel J., *The Exploring Spirit: America and the World, Then and Now*, Random House (1976), pp. 87-88.

3. Hillburn, Wiley W., Jr., "Fragments," *The Times*, Oct. 25, 1992.

4. Jung, Carl G., *Memories, Dreams, Reflections*, Vintage Books (1989), p. 244.

5. Jung, Carl G., editor, *Man and His Symbols*, including "Approaching the Unconscious" by Jung and "Ancient Myths and Modern Man" by Joseph L Henderson, Doubleday & Company, Inc. (1964) pp.55, 107.

6. Hayakawa, S. I., *Symbol, Status and Personality*, Harcourt, Brace &World, Inc. (1958), pp. 131-132.

7. Kast, Verena, *The Dynamics of Symbols, Fundamentals of Jungian Psychotherapy*, pp. 128-130.

8. Langer, Susanne K., *Philosophy in a New Key: A Study in the Symbolism of Reason, Rite and Art*, Harvard University Press (3d ed. 1957), p. 41.

9. Lederer, Richard, *The Miracle of Language*, Pocket Books (1991), p. xvii

10. Ritchie, A.D., *The Natural History of the Mind*, London: Longmans, Green & Co. (1936).

11. Whittick, Arnold, *Symbols, Signs and Their Meaning*, Charles T. Bramford Company (1960), p. 3.

12. Whitmont, Edward C., *The Symbolic Quest, Basic Concepts of Analytical Psychology*, G.P. Putman's Sons (1969), p. 219.

Suggested Reading

Bergson, Henri, *Creative Evolution*, translated by Arthur Mitchell, Greenwood Press (1975).

Blair, Lawrence, *Rhythms of Vision: The Changing Patterns of Belief*, Schocken Books (1976).

Campbell, Joseph, *The Power of Myth*, Doubleday (1988).

Ellwood, Robert, *Theosophy: A Modern Expression of the Wisdom of the Ages*, The Theosophical Publishing House (1987).

Grudin, Robert, *The Grace of Great Things: Creativity and Innovation*, Ticknor & Fields (1990).

Harman, Willis, Ph.D. and Rheingold, Howard, *Higher Creativity: Liberating the Unconscious for Breakthrough Insights*, Jeremy P. Tarcher (1984).

Jung, Carl, *Psychology and Alchemy, Collected Works*, vol. 12.

Pascal, Eugene, *Jung to Live By: A Guide to the Practical Application of Jungian Principles for Everyday Life*, Warner Books (1992).

Progoff, Ira, *The Symbolic and the Real*, McGraw-Hill Book Co. (1963).

Ronner, John, *Seeing Your Future: A Modern Look at Prophecy and Prediction*, Mamre Press (1990).

Segaller, Stephen and Berger, Merrill, *The Wisdom of the Dream: The World of C. G. Jung*, Shambhala (1990).

Thomas, Henry and Thomas, Dana Lee, *Living Biographies of Great Philosophers*, Garden City Books (1959).

About the Author

Mary Jo McCabe, an attractive and vivacious wife, mother and otherwise "normal" person, has been trance-channeling since 1981. Her teaching and interpretive skills are enhanced by a group of entities whom she refers to as "the Guides." Through her, they exhibit love, humor, and a deep caring for humanity.

Mary Jo's special insight led her to establish the McCabe Institute, which is dedicated to helping people get in touch with their inner voice, or Higher Self. In group sessions, guided meditations and retreats, and in private, Mary Jo provides personal information and guidance on how to know yourself and better understand your purpose in life.